Will of God

Will of God

The Formation of the Faithful

Kenneth Francis

Published by Seven Virtues

Anxiety is the Enemy of Wisdom

United States
First Edition, 2025

This is a nonfiction work. Scripture quotations are taken from various translations of the Holy Bible, used under fair use guidelines for educational and devotional purposes.
All rights for the respective Bible translations are held by their copyright holders.

ISBN: 979-8-9990640-0-4

Cover design by Kenneth Francis
Interior formatting by Kenneth Francis

Published by Seven Virtues
Anxiety is the Enemy of Wisdom

Printed in the United States of America
First Edition

For permissions or inquiries, contact:
7evenV@gmail.com

Table of Contents

Preface

Since childhood, my favorite forms of entertainment have been fiction and fantasy, especially Sci-Fi shows. However, as an adult, I am never comfortable reading fiction. In literature, it conflicts with my way of thinking. Additionally, I would enjoy reading something that genuinely interests me and captures my attention, but I do not particularly like reading just for the sake of it. Nevertheless, I believe that God, in His providence, has always guided me in my learning as He prepared me to hear the truth. Still, I needed exposure beyond my formal education to gain a deeper understanding, conduct investigative analysis, distinguish between the truth and its different aspects, and tell apart the God-breathed Word from human explanation.

As a new believer, I had an immense thirst for the Word of God. That thirst launched a quest not only for the Scriptures themselves but also for literature surrounding them, and the knowledge and discernment needed to divide them rightly. I believe God orchestrated this journey, with books that appeared at pivotal moments, helping me learn to compare, examine, and evaluate texts, only to disappear when their time was up. Four books, two before my regeneration and two after, significantly shaped how I recognize truth and filter information.

Before my salvific experience, my culture and limited exposure shaped my search for truth, and an attraction to the Rastafarian sect. Although tempted by the freedoms it offered, I also admired certain aspects that supported its claim of being part of the Nazarite sect while still aligning with my subconscious Judeo-Christian roots.

Although I recognized that Rastafarian was pretty flawed, being completely subjective and relative (sometimes just plain hypocritical, prejudiced, and self-indulgent), I believed, as a true Nazarene: adhering to the Nazarite vow as it was prescribed in the Old Testament (at least to an "acceptable contemporary version"), it would lead me on a path to righteousness. So, I bought a book on the subject (Rastafarian) to understand what I believed in. After reading that book, I was just as disconnected as before; there was no transcendence, no core truth, and no indication pointing to any source of curiosity, much less a source of support.

The argument for Selassie's divinity was that he was a descendant of the throne of David through the Queen of Sheba's visit to Solomon. II. His name is Tafari, which means "King Creator," and he was given the title "King of Kings of all Ethiopia and Lord of all Lords" by the Queen of England. III. Miraculous events are said to have occurred in his life: one story describes a swarm of bees helping him win a battle against Mussolini, which, if true, would be consistent with the life of a believer in the office of a King. The point here is not to verify facts but to emphasize the danger of such assumptions. Giving titles or divine qualities to earthly rulers, who are supposed to serve as a light of truth to the masses, can be misleading. This is especially true considering how many times they have been falsely presented, such as through the distortion of Christianity, pagan influences, slavery, colonization, and more.

Furthermore, men work relentlessly to hide and replace the Word of God with their corrupt agendas and the appearance of success, which the enemy also exploited through our betrayal and distrust to foster disbelief in the truth. Additionally, our ethnic pride has been demonized.

Accepting the beliefs fed to us often feels like a psychological conflict and self-betrayal. This is also a key reason why many of African descent either believe in or feel more spiritually connected to Muhammad than to Jesus. The messengers and messages seem to align more closely with our culture and ethnicity, and the antagonist introduced our faithful Lord under a false guise and ethnicity. Even if this is not objectively true, it remains a cultural reality. For most of us who have been set free by God's call, without being Spirit-led through sound biblical teaching, there is still a psychological bondage of feeling inferior or caught in ethnic debates.

The two-volume autobiography of Haile Selassie I was another book that helped shape my approach and discernment of the truth before my conversion. Unlike the theological claims of Rastafarianism, he describes his Christian Walk, his religious practices, and his yearly pilgrimage to Jerusalem as acts of devotion to his faith. It aligned with the life of a believer and a leader of his nation, suggesting that God may have worked in his life. Rastafarians pointed out this as proof that he was more than just a man. However, he never claimed to be the messiah or the second coming, not even in a distant sense. It is ironic how we can interpret a sign or wonder during rare moments and attribute it to the highest of ranks—way beyond merit (second coming)—while ignoring or disbelieving the countless signs and wonders in the Bible and the lives of believers, which are meant to inspire belief in the Lord Jesus Christ.

In the two years before my regeneration, I desperately searched to fill a void that consumed me. I looked in books and religions. From Rastafarian beliefs to my version of Judaism, I was also curious about Buddhism. Then, one day, the Holy Spirit took hold of my heart. In the following months, I was isolated, reading the Word, fasting, and praying. The meaning of those books was still as unclear and unknown to me. The significance only became clear after the Holy Spirit started guiding my learning, helping me understand how to distinguish between facts and truth, and allowing me to identify the root of a text concerning a principle rather than what falls off a theoretical cliff.

In retrospect, these books were not the only tools God used; several unexpected texts acted as catalysts. One example is a 1930s Cambridge textbook, Text Matter 3, which I discovered shortly before my conversion. In a parenthetical discussion on Plato's Allegory of the Cave, the dialogue between a philosopher and his protégé resonated with me. I realized I had been living in that cave. After returning to Grenada after ten years abroad, I found that my life had been a shadow of anger, frustration, and helplessness until then. This realization coincided with the deepest spiritual battle of my life. Strangely, the book disappeared shortly after I was saved.

Another turning point occurred during my visits to the National Library of Grenada, where I discovered Engineering and Humanities by Schaub and Dickinson (University of Florida, 1987). Tucked inside was an essay by Karl Richard Pavlovic: "Making, Doing, and Thinking." In a broader discussion on technology, history, and ethics, Pavlovic offered a reflection that struck me like a wave:

"The irony is that people who have experienced the efficacy of rational discussion, i.e., precisely those people already persuaded, would be the only beneficiaries, for those people who are not so acquainted, i.e., those whom I would hope to persuade, would in all likelihood remain unpersuaded." – Karl Richard Pavlovic.

This statement struck another chord of frustration; during my "eye-opening," I felt torn between a convicted conscience and the world, and my approaches to people were often met with either offense or mockery. The conflict in my dilemma was, "If I concluded this statement to be true, then it is pointless." Indeed, it was pointless in my natural wrestling. As I grappled with feelings of human disconnection and helplessness, I discovered the answer in my own salvation experience. The words of Jesus became clear to me: "What is impossible with man is possible with God." This brings me to the first impactful book after Being Born Again: True Spirituality by Francis Schaeffer; the journey of discovering it is even more significant than the book itself. Shortly after my conversion, the Holy Spirit directed me, turn by turn, to a bookstore to buy this book. The irony is that, 15 years later, I now begin to understand the full implications and effects of that experience of discovering the book and the book itself.

Section 1

I beseech you therefore, brethren, by the mercies of God, that ye present your bodies a living sacrifice, holy, acceptable unto God, *which is* your reasonable service. And be not conformed to this world: but be ye transformed by the renewing of your mind, that ye may prove what *is* that good, and acceptable, and perfect, will of God.
- Romans 12:1,2 (KJV)

Chapter 1

Distinguishing Truth

How I Found "True Spirituality."

If you have read the preface, let us pick up from there. Soon after my conversion, I woke up each day amazed by what was happening to me. Sometimes, I would visit my "happy place"—the hill where I used to fly kites during Easter and summer vacations as a kid. There, I learned to sit and talk to the Holy Spirit. At other times, I would feel the Holy Spirit's voice prompting me while sitting in the shack where I got saved.

During these sacred moments, the Holy Spirit sometimes gave me specific instructions. For instance, He once prompted me, "Go to your sister's house," and then, "turn on the TV." This led me to discover a Christian broadcasting network. For the first time, I understood that Christians worldwide are filled with the indwelling of the Spirit. (It was one of the Manpower conferences where T.D. Jakes preached "The Limp That Will Not Leave.") On other occasions, I felt the physical promptings to "Look up!" just in time to see a large, hairy spider retreating between the rafters, with a variety of similar promptings occurring at other times, to help me conquer my fear of spiders.

However, that day felt different. I sensed a deeper purpose behind the prompting, even though I did not know the reason or the destination. I only came to understand where I was headed when I arrived there.

That day, I got up, dressed, and followed the prompt to take a bus into the city. After getting off the bus, I listened to that still, small voice, which directed me with instructions like "Take this street," "Turn right and then left," and so on until I ended up on a short, dead-end street. The prompting led me to the second-to-last building on that street, where I discovered a Christian bookstore.

Once inside the bookstore, I was prompted to buy Francis Schaeffer's "True Spirituality." I believe it was the only copy of that book in the store. The entire process, from leaving my house that morning to purchasing the book, was guided by prompts at each step, even though it seemed like a mere impulse. Notably, before that day, I was unaware of that bookstore's existence.

Regarding distinguishing truth or the authenticity of scripture, I was unaware of the natural dilemma involving philosophical predispositions and epistemology—the human tendency to hold specific views and attitudes, along with the debates over the scope of knowledge and the rationale of our faith, even among some Christians, despite God bearing witness to His word. This concept had not occurred to me. From the day of my first discernible encounter with the Holy Spirit on August 3rd, 2002, and for the next couple of years, I was taught by Him. I diligently engaged with the Scriptures daily, prayed fervently, and practiced regular fasting. The Word and Spirit indeed led my life.

For example, I went back to that same bookstore, and there it was, "The Mystery of God's Will (What Does He Want for me?)" - Charles R Swindoll. My eyes lit up; I thought, "This is the book I have been looking for. If I can only know the Will of God for my life." So, I went home and started reading the book, and that internal voice said, "Do not read that." I shrugged it off as a voice in the background, yielding to the temptation of that knowledge. Nevertheless, He allowed me to read a few pages in His mercy, perhaps to impress the significance on my mind better, and then was physically prompted to stop. After this experience, I began to write seriously because that book had nothing to do with the will of God, but rather a rash explanation of human behavior and the rationalization of events like the Kennedy assassination. And yes, I said I was physically prompted to stop. In other places, I described the painful prompting or displeasure on the right side of my head or brain (which I assumed was a warning or discernment of evil) and the acute, pleasurable pain on the left side, which I interpreted as discerning good. I never understood why, but I assumed the Spirit of God used this method to get my attention when my hearing was dull or disobedient. Even in my writing, when I am not fully yielded and begin to stray by hearing other thoughts and ideas, He would use that to steer me back.

That book and that experience ignited my intense urgency and zeal to write this book. I needed to make at least a genuine attempt to address the misleading information surrounding the most crucial topic ever— "The Will of God." It infuriated me that someone would take such a serious subject and express such rash opinions.

Concerning interpretation and popular doctrines

With hermeneutics, the concern of man's interpretation, and its various schools of thought, I did not have a problem either. Although I was not well-versed in doctrine, I began to study scripture through naked inquiry and a hunger for truth, often praying beforehand for understanding. I received it as best as my faculties allowed. Back then, my limited knowledge was less relevant than it is today. In my writing, the Holy Spirit sometimes gave me the scripture and helped me interpret it. Sometimes, after I write, He reminds me of the corresponding scripture text, prompting me to look it up. Other times, the needed scripture verse is unfamiliar, and He provides me with the book, chapter, and verses. This is amazing because I find it challenging to remember chapters, verses, dates, and so on.

For most of my first 15 years as a believer, I studied the Bible, learned to interpret scripture, and lived a spiritual life while adhering to the more popular denominations and some non-denominational platforms. I experienced growth and success in discipline, devotion, doctrine, and faith, but I had little revelation. Under most of their teachings, my walk was more about effort and less about grace in growth. The emphasis was always on behavioral modification, personality, and "effort faith." They would tell you to be spiritual to overcome your sinful nature. However, the demonstration and presentation were filtered through personality selection and discipline growth, with little to no inward transformation I had first experienced.

Here is what I mean. God is no respecter of persons. God will change you, provided you yield to His transformation. His sovereign hand will humble you regardless of your personality traits, temperament, and upbringing. The Holy Spirit will enter and work a transformation within you. You will experience a Spirit-filled life characterized by growth and transformation, even amid your failures and trials, as long as you are genuinely repentant and abide in the truth. However, it must stem from a genuine hunger and acknowledgment of spiritual poverty, leading you to a place of earnest seeking, where we should naturally be as newborn babes in Christ, held in the unwavering, loving arms of the Holy Spirit.

The problem arises when our primary focus shifts to doctrinal and character discipline, causing us to lose the individual footprint of our walk with God, which is rooted in His Word and Spirit within us, rather than simply engaging in traditional, religious, and devotional gatherings.

As part of many denominational congregations, I have discovered that approving men based on their charisma and performance often leaves behind those who genuinely desire change. They are pushed out due to personal struggles or unmet expectations, while some are elevated with false assurance.

For all these years, I had misunderstood it because I was holding on to the idea that somehow got lodged in my psyche—my corporate worship experience and my leader's following should be prioritized over my intimacy with God. Many teachers have fervently emphasized this. Our interactive skills and personality traits were taught to be the mark of our spirituality, validated by community fellowship. We were told, as sheep, that we are incapable of understanding more than our spiritual head. At times, when my hunger and conscience conflicted with what I was taught, my confusion would hinder my persistence or consistency in church.

Back to the present

Moral failures, doctrinal struggles, personality deficiencies, and a lack of cultivated discipline led me back to that place of desperate contrition. I recalled that time, shortly after my conversion, when a fire burned in my belly; it was pure euphoria. With prayer and fasting, I begged God to give me what I had back then, to which the Holy Spirit brought me full circle. He directed me right back to Francis Schaeffer's "True Spirituality," and then I moved on to A.W. Tozer's "Pursuit of God" and "How to be filled with the Holy Spirit." No exaggeration, the fire ignited. The first scripture to explode in me was, "He who the Son sets free is free indeed."

I went from monitoring my current weaknesses around the clock to an unclenched peace and self-control I had not enjoyed in years.

It is not about the books and their doctrine and theology, but about their ability to shift your mind to grasp the truth and walk in a new reality or disclosure. I continued to revise the doctrines of the faith through the books of Schaeffer, Tozer, etc., and other denominational teachings. I would often listen to men like R.C. Sproul and Ravi Zacharias. Ligonier Ministry and its affiliates have also become a staple in my current pursuit of Reformed Theology.

A while back, a friend introduced me to Bob Utley on YouTube, which led me to "How to Read the Bible for All Its Worth" by Gordon Fee and Douglas Stuart. This book changed how I approach studying scripture and related literature. Primarily, a good book in light of doctrine should help remove the shades from your eyes. Most of our churches are arbitrarily biased toward a so-called "school of thought," and our trust and loyalty chain us in ignorance. I recall being told, as a congregation, things like "we believe in election and not predestination," or which Bible translation not to use. For example, we were told that a particular translation was less trustworthy than the other, which is the house translation. I have come to understand that each translation has its advantages, but most mainstream translations are generally reliable. Using multiple translations is best; various book criteria can help guide you to a proper investigation. I have discovered that a study bible, such as The Hebrew–Greek Key Word Study Bible, is one of the best study tools.

"How to Read the Bible for All It's Worth" also explains hermeneutics and our need to learn and practice exegesis. Aside from that, the few people who previously explained those terms remained obscure, referring to their purpose as an elite skill of the clergy. Another book to consider is "Knowing Scripture" by R C Sproul. It would also be helpful to explore his archive.

Opinion:
- I am perplexed because I have read these books, and when I look at Christianity, I realize that some of us are so far from the mark; it is heart-wrenching. The prologues and introductions of some of these writers make claims of "guarantee" and their prophetic insights into a move on the convicted heart, which initially caught me off guard, but they are right. Those books that emphasize and expound the scripture (not all hit the nail on the head) immediately move you with conviction. If they do not accomplish that, you are likely not regenerated. Otherwise, they urge you to change your internal position and walk before a real God. Alternatively, as Paul says, you should take heed to examine yourself and see if you are in the Faith.

The phrase 'the individual footprint of our walk with God' highlights your intimacy with God, which I believe is essential. This applies to any meaningful relationship. My experiences with God, which began at my salvation, continue through an ever-reviving journey with Him to this day. Very few things outside of this intimacy have spurred my growth throughout my Christian Walk: one was my unique encounters with individuals in every city I moved to; there would always be someone God led me to, someone who understood my situation and could relate to my relationship with God. The second aspect involves my writing—it is consistently sparked by concerns over fallacies or misunderstandings propagated among Believers. For instance, the book I bought on the Will of God in 2003 was a total misconception of His will. However, it is more concerning that the Bible is routinely overlooked in favor of other sources in a desperate search for His will. As a nearly year-old believer, I entered churches yearning for a corporate experience with God, only to realize the errors and foolishness being taught and practiced within these structures. Yet, I felt powerless—how can a new believer, just a few months old in Christ, correct people who have been in the faith for 20 to 30 years? These experiences marked my early spiritual growth.

As I grew, the Spirit of God taught me how to interpret and understand Scripture in its literal sense and the principles it conveys, not just for information and instruction. I believe He began laying the foundation two years before my conversion, using texts such as Plato, Text Matter, and Karl Pavlovic, among others. These works significantly sharpened my deductive reasoning. However, moving forward, the Holy Spirit would change the approach; He would illuminate Scripture through contemplation and then guide me to the text for mental recognition.

I referenced somewhere in Chapter six the most profound experience I have ever had: being pulled into the text of Genesis in a trance-like state, where I experienced a revelation of the Genesis text of creation (Genesis 1:2). Part of what I retained from that experience, which I could articulate, was that eternity made room for our natural existence; a piece of in-existence or void was created within the eternal existence of God, centered on time and the foundational waters from which He formed natural existence – this is my best interpretation as I experienced it.

Returning to myself, I could not wait to write everything I observed. However, when I picked up the pen and paper, there was very little I could express in words. Then the Holy Spirit said, "What is understood is written so that what cannot be written may be understood." I took this to mean that He provides us with what our natural faculties can grasp in the written word, enabling Him to reveal what cannot be comprehended naturally. This is the essence of faith: "The substance of things hoped for, the evidence of the things not seen" – believing God by trusting beyond our natural comprehension and living according to reason and logic. In faith, our hope is anchored in heaven. We trust what the word says beyond the natural laws of observation and our natural understanding, acknowledging His otherness, assured, as if with tangible evidence, of what He says, and expecting beyond visible proof, whether for present needs or future promises.

The need arises to understand beyond my limited education as the years pass. I listened to many messages, studied, and finally, the frustration set in during a systematic theology class I took at the church I attended. I felt stagnant because the leader required us to regurgitate only what he had taught. They instructed us in the basic Word through their interpretation without allowing us to recognize the organic nature of the truth. They stifled our curiosity and potential for illumination. Through all this, I now understand that God, by His providence, has measured my stagnation just as He has measured my progress for proper growth.

Another trigger that motivated my continuation and the second part of this book was that both types of "special individual encounters"- personal and spiritual—were involved. We met when I returned to New York in 2008/2009. I greatly respected her walk as a believer and genuinely cared about her. I believe God used our friendship, which may not have been a burden, except that I thought someone I cared about was at risk of peril due to the "current blindness." She fervently expressed concern about the inerrancy of various Bible translations and their attempts to manipulate and corrupt scripture. As a result, she zealously safeguarded herself against what she believed to be the corruption of scripture by prioritizing spiritual experiences and devotion to an obscure translation imposed by their leaders. At the time, my doctrinal scroll began to highlight "heresy" next to her name - in all honesty, in my zeal, I was ready to cut her off had it not been for my own experiences. I believe in the experiential nature of our spiritual walk when subservient to scripture, which aligns with mainstream translations.

My zeal sparked a debate within me about a personal experiential walk with God and the authority of scripture in its sacerdotal and congregational framework, as it is taught by many to be essential mediators, which conflicted with my own experience. I did not realize then that the error was in my distinguishing – a personal experiential walk with God and the authority of scripture are totally and coherently synonymous. Still, the errors of hierarchical teaching have shaped our thinking. We are taught that the clergy gives us access and still veils us from the Holy of Holies. Neither sacerdotal, clergical, nor congregational mandates dictate the framework of scriptural authority, but where applicable, they follow the guidelines of scriptural authority. It is, therefore, the duty of every believer to have a personal experiential walk with God, bound by the authority of the Word, witnessed by His Spirit. And the clerical and congregational administration of the Body will take its form.

Chapter 2

The Reverence and Wonder of His Recognition

Aside from religious and ritual settings, my earliest awareness of God's presence occurred between the ages of six and ten. We were engaged in our usual summer adventures as kids, whether trying to access someone's property or teasing an unsuspecting animal. I remember we gathered in a semicircle against a hedge or fence, with me at the back of the group. What left a lasting impression that day was a sudden feeling, a realization that God was watching me. I paused, looked up as if God had caught my attention, and said, "I see you, and you know better than this." Without telling my friends, I stepped back from the activity. Ironically, there was no shame or fear in knowing that He saw me. Instead, I felt a sense of reverence, awe, and acceptance. Yes, I felt conviction, but His recognition brought me reverence and acceptance in wonder.

As a young boy, I enjoyed attending church and participating in religious events and activities. However, as I grew past twelve, I moved further and further away from religion and the so-called things of God. As an adult, it reached a point where I lifted my fist at Him in defiance. After a while, I became increasingly frustrated with an unbearable emptiness. In my search to fill that void, I tried Rastafarianism and its flavor of the Nazarite sect, then shifted more toward Judaism, attempting to follow the teachings of the Old Testament. Still left with that emptiness, I became curious about Buddhism. However, in August 2002, I had a profound encounter with the Holy Spirit, marked by a noticeable conversion or regeneration. From then on, my life underwent drastic changes. For one, during the first two years or so as a believer, I was taught by the Holy Spirit. I began to experience an unquenchable thirst for the word of God and its illuminating power, which revealed insights, fostered consistent conviction, and led to daily growth.

As I began to fellowship with the saints, moving from place to place, I joined local congregations for worship. However, regardless of the denomination, any address of sin among the congregation often brought condemnation, shame, and guilt. While guilt is necessary for acknowledging sin, shame tainted my soul as a curse. Guilt with remorse brings repentance, but shame condemns me with a stained conscience. This hindered my ability to partake in holy things. In turn, I tried to get and live right by my efforts. However, performance-based efforts seemed to satisfy my conscience momentarily, and even so, just before men. My performance could not redeem or sanctify my past or current actions; therefore, the guilt and shame remained.

When guilt pushes our performance to attain righteousness, it leads to a religious experience bound by laws. As preached, we are free by doctrinal decree, the clearly defined tenets of our faith, as received by the message of truth. The gospel of our salvation! Sealed with the promised Holy Spirit. I knew Jesus died for my sins, and in the gracious clarity of His Spirit, I enjoyed that liberty. However, as I said, in congregation after congregation, in our religious engagements, I was made to feel the need to do penance for those same sins and, therefore, my salvation.

Do not get me wrong, when we sin, there must be genuine internal remorse and repentance, and sometimes restitution. Not for an account of redemption or to restore your relationship with God, but rather to continue our sanctification. However, often, instead of our conscience and remorse serving as a means of setting boundaries, I have found that institutions use them to keep us in a state of guilt and shame. They demand constant proof of our worthiness by legalistic requirements.

On the other hand, some churches put their trust in universal grace and the confessional nature of our faith. In these congregations, there was no conviction, and the fruit of change or sanctification through the struggle against sin was lacking.

I recall sitting in such congregations and discerning the grief of the Holy Spirit through that unpleasant sensation I mentioned elsewhere. Whereby I would be prompted or directed. In such cases, I would regain my peace with God after leaving the congregation to a solitary sanctity. It appears I was better off by myself, and in some of those instances, I was.

This was because most of these congregations were either ignorant of the truth and the gospel of their salvation or unsaved. Therefore, any serious attempt to address sin was usually played out by man's application of the law and conscience. Meanwhile, the true conviction of the Holy Spirit was sidestepped or overlooked by some penitent act we were told to perform to get right with God. During these periods, many of my actions or inactions were motivated by shame or pride rather than the liberty of a new agency, as with my initial conversion and growth, a will of desire that comes by His recognition in awe and reverence. It had its share of doubts and valleys, but was accompanied by His comfort and assurance of mountain-top experiences. In comparison, most of my maturing years in the fellowship were a vicious cycle of guilt and struggle with sin and mistakes.

"God is spirit, and his worshipers must worship in the Spirit and in truth."

Any real experience or worship of God is unfacilitated by empty rituals and laws, except that it is inherent to faith or our salvation; it must be spiritual. He never provided meritorious means or qualifiers by which we must climb to him (neither on this mountain nor in Jerusalem). However, institutions have insisted on using the church organization to interpret our relationship through legal and meritorious works. As a result, trained to see the institutions synonymous with the body of Christ, we try to reverence and seek the acceptance we initially felt from His recognition through meritorious works. Except we find shame and guilt, causing us to shrink from the wonder of interest we once had in getting to know Him.

What happened between then and now? When the institutions we are a part of are merely substitutions and not intrinsically a representation and reflection of His body, we lose the light of His love and find ourselves in this dark corridor of the unknown, where reverence turns to fear and acceptance into anxiety. This disconnect is often the source of longing and confusion over God's will, stemming from the loss of consensus within the Church—a consensus that has already been clearly stated in Scripture. To "Love the Lord your God with all your heart, soul, strength and mind, and your neighbor as yourself." (Luke 10:27). Or "Keep on loving one another as brothers and sisters." (Heb. 13:1 NIV).

If we fulfill our responsibilities in our natural relationships, we are already pleasing God to the point where some have unknowingly entertained angels.

God never expected us to find His will by climbing an institutional or structural ladder. He has a structural calling, but we often confuse it with positional authority in the church, and we impose that authority as a ladder to reach God.

The will of God, as summarized by Jesus, concerning the law. Love, your Neighbors

When the lawyer in Luke 10 asked Jesus, "Who is my neighbor?" He told him the story of a man attacked by robbers, only to receive help from a Samaritan. He made it clear that your neighbor is the one who chose to love you as they love themselves. In this context, the neighbor is a verb, referring to the one who acts on your behalf, rather than just a noun, a member of a neighborhood's proximity or residence; a true neighbor is the one who has an inherent love for their fellow man. That was the test to which each of the men encountering the wounded man was faced, including the priest and the Levite. However, they were not willing to inconvenience themselves to help him. If they were in his shoes, what would they consider compassionate? They would expect their rescue to be a priority for their neighbor. So, are they now willing to give this man the same priority? By doing that, they would love him as they would themselves and fulfill the terms of a neighbor, as did the Samaritan. Your neighbor is the fulfillment of an act of love and, therefore, righteous. Thus, Jesus said, there are only two commandments: Love the Lord your God with all your soul, heart, and mind, and love your neighbor as yourself. Be righteous with God and with man.

The text did not refer to the Samaritan as the "Good Samaritan," but he has inherited the prefix by tradition. Inherently, "good" is a title of righteousness. Jesus made it clear when a certain man called him "good master" - he asked him, "Why do you call me good? No one is good – except God." The lawyer in Luke 10's initial question was, "What must I do to inherit eternal life?" Christ asked him, "What is written in the law?" He summarized it, "Love the Lord your God with all your heart and with all your soul and with your strength and with all your mind and love your neighbor as yourself. Jesus said, "You are right, do this, and you will live." Then he asks, "Who is my neighbor?" Ironically, at the end of the story, Jesus asks, "Which of those three was a neighbor to the man who fell into the hands of the robbers?" He did not ask which of his neighbors did their duty, but who was a neighbor to him?

From the beginning, man has been asking essentially the same question. How do we please God? Which is the greatest commandment of them all? What is the will of God? The problem is that we have never been satisfied with the answer. Originally, man had a truly corporeal mystical relationship with God before Adam fell, but now, it is only through the mystery of Christ. Instead of accepting our natural state, we keep trying to rebuild the Tower of Babel, fixated on that mystical experience, by even trying to get Him to come down to our will. In the Old Testament, they continually asked Jesus for a sign, and

He responded that a wicked and perverse generation asked for a sign. Today, we still ask for signs. We neglect the commandment to love God in heaven by demonstrating that love to our fellow men on earth. We continue to ask for a mystical experience of His will and supernatural blessings on earth. We often expect him to manifest his mystery in the form of miracles and supernatural wealth, such as cash, houses, land, or prominent gifts, not realizing that often, when we ask of his will, it is self-motivated. These things are blessings, and He does bless, but they are just blessings. The whole earth is full of His blessings. We plant and tend and rip a harvest, but we sow in righteousness so that the earth may rip a blessing of who we are.

Love one another.

What if Jesus said, Love the Lord your God by loving one another?

In a way, he did say that. He said, "If you love me, you will keep my commandments." And then he said, "This is my commandment, that you love one another, just as I have loved you."

So, in essence, the will of God, as demonstrated in Jesus' practical application, is that we love one another and love our neighbor as ourselves. However, when He commanded us to love one another, He commanded that we do it just as He has loved us. Our love for one another is a love we receive from Him and is a bit different from loving our neighbor. The "one another" Jesus speaks of are those who are in Him because, in Him, we are separated from the world as our dwelling place. However, the love of our neighbor is among the whole world, whether of ourselves or in the world, because we are required to love regardless.

"If anyone loves Me, he will follow My word; and My Father will love him, and We will come to him and make Our dwelling with him."(John 14:23) – This dwelling is the indwelling of the Holy Spirit in every true believer unto eternal life, which is wrought in Christ by what we often call, "born again," "saved," "regenerated," etc., albeit an actual supernatural event in time and space, and its corporative nature of the Church as the body of Christ which include all believers, among

whom we love one another as he loved us. Without the indwelling of the Holy Spirit, you will never have fellowship with us because only true believers can have fellowship with one another.

That which was from the beginning, which we have heard, which we have seen with our own eyes, which we have looked upon and touched with our hands, concerning the word of life – the life was made manifest, and we have seen it, and testify to it and proclaim to you the eternal life, which was <u>with</u> the Father and was made manifest to us – that which we have seen and heard we proclaim also to you, so that you too may have fellowship <u>with</u> us; and indeed our fellowship is with the Father and with his Son Jesus Christ. - 1 John 1-3

Chapter 3

Quest by Anxiety

Beloved, the gifts of grace are not immediately enjoyed by new believers. Coming to Christ, we are saved by a true union with him. But it is by remaining in that union that we further receive the purity, the joy, the power, and the blessedness which are stored up in him for his people.
-    Charles H. Spurgeon.

The search of a young believer is often shrouded in misunderstandings about God's will. Instinctively, we know there is a personal instructive aspect, which we all initially say is "the Will of God for my life." However, this is often a broader concept that is yet to be grasped and developed by our faculties.

The implication is that a subjective aspect, such as a self-willed faith, will reveal God's will for our lives. It is indeed a personal grace, but the problem lies in our self-centeredness. We tend to focus on ourselves instead of God and our neighbors, reminiscent of the Garden of Eden temptation to be like God. Though this pursuit is sincere, it is like a new computer not yet connected to the network; it is operational but unable to look beyond itself.

Romans 12:1-3 says.

I beseech you brethren, by the mercies of God that ye present your bodies a living sacrifice, holy, acceptable unto God, (which is) your reasonable service. And be not conformed to this world: but be transformed by the renewing of your mind, that ye may know what is that good and acceptable and perfect will of God.

One of the biggest misconceptions in the Church, especially among young believers, is the idea of God's will. We often think, "If I only knew that specific thing or mission." Maybe for that season, year, day, or even my entire life. Then I could walk in His will and not worry about disobeying or messing up." Let us assume that His will is some accomplished goal or specific mission for our lives. If it were revealed to us (still driven by anxiety), would you be able to achieve it? Also, if His will had been revealed to you, assuming it is some purpose for this life, and you are rooted in virtue and patience, would our limited or temporary lifespan (or the disposal of the flesh) and its restricted capacity allow us to fully understand the eternal will of God, much less fulfill it?

He has called us to that fulfillment, but our faculties accommodate such revelation as a reflection of light, not in its propagation. However, to reflect such refulgence, that light must first induce us; there must first be an effective influence and resemblance (induced resemblance) of Him, but in us, it is impossible. In our search, we naturally ask, "What do we have to do or achieve?" There is nothing we can do ourselves to reflect such glory; it is beyond our ability to grasp and carry, which brings us back to this induced resemblance.

The Scripture says, *"The Son is the image of the invisible God"* (Colossians 1:15), and *"the radiance of God's glory and the exact representation of His being"* (Hebrews 1:3).

Our resemblance or representation of this glory is Christ in us. When we say, "Christ in us" or "in Christ," we often think of ourselves as reflecting Christ in our character, but let us think more of Christ reflecting His character in us. Something that is done in us rather than an outcome of our virtue. Ironically, our faith's two most evident marks are "death" and "grace." They exist beyond our power, in our total helplessness and complete enablement, allowing us to do what we otherwise could not. We acknowledge this in our religion through rituals, but overlook it in our core beliefs and daily lives. By that token, the one who lives forever died so that we who have a sentence of death can live forever by His grace. So, when Paul described his service to God, he said,

"I am glad when I suffer for you in my body, for I am participating in the suffering of Christ that continue for His body the church." ... This message was kept secret for centuries and generations past, but now it has been revealed to God's people.

For God wanted them to know that the riches and glory of Christ are for you Gentiles too. And this is the secret: Christ lives in you. This gives you assurance of sharing his glory. Colossians 1:24-27 NLT.

What does all this mean?

Deep within us, there is a gap marked by both a sense of loss and a longing. However, in our sinful nature, this gap is misinterpreted as a desire for enlightenment—an urge to know more or to be near or included among those with special knowledge. It drives some of us to seek secret revelations or cling to those who claim such insights or display special gifts. This is the root of pagan worship and cult behavior, fueled by our pride to ascend to the heavens and be like the Most High God.

As new believers, suspicion of this other world has become reality, but not in the way we once imagined. The enlightenment we seek is not an ascent but a realization of our descent and a blow to our natural pride; there is no self-enlightenment. Lucifer, the "morning star," tried to ascend to God's throne, and Christ saw him fall from heaven like lightning. When Satan tempted Adam and Eve against God's will, he said, *"For God knows that when you eat from it your eyes will be opened, and you will be like God, knowing good and evil"* (Genesis 3:5). And from that temptation came death.

So, the innate gap is not a sense of hope but a profound sense of loss—the memory of separation from God's glory, just as Lucifer was cast out. Now, as believers, we have a new living hope—not a blueprint for a self-willed pursuit, but the assurance of sharing His glory again, proclaimed through the power of Christ, even as this gap is being filled. "This is the secret: Christ lives in you."

Therefore, our actual contribution is merely as an object moved by the hand of grace or providence.

Ephesians 2:8 says.

For by grace are ye saved through faith; and not of ourselves, (it is) the gift of God: Not of works, lest any man should boast.

Remember, our salvation was an Isolated work unaided by our virtue and desire, no matter our zeal and natural goodwill. It is **by grace,** through faith...a gift (the faith is not even of us, it is of Christ).

I do not frustrate the grace of God: For if righteousness comes by (works) the law, then Christ died in vain. - Galatians 2:21

From Faith to Obedience

This book is a witness to this process. When I was first prompted to write, it seemed the opportunities never arose—namely, a quiet, undisturbed place or time after quiet meditation, since that is the condition I have learned to write under. However, I have been convicted of disobedience. While I reason with God based on my circumstances, "I am taking care of two kids by myself, and other issues that would pop up did not exactly allow me time to do it, sometimes even at night."

I needed an environment that would help me think clearly. That is not bad, but my reasoning would frustrate the grace of God. I would sometimes do this when the Holy Spirit gave me a text to write, which often did not make sense until the context or paragraph was complete. I would try to reason it out, only to find myself wrestling against the insight of the Holy Spirit. So, God, in His mercy, would work it out so that I had no choice but to write amidst the chaos of life's circumstances. In the process, God, in His long-suffering, taught me to walk in obedience rather than try to validate the wisdom of God through my reasoning. After seeing the finished product, I realized how foolish I had been—I could not reason out those things.

I am not only substantially delivered from the burden of my own "wisdom" and the power I thought I needed to have over my circumstances, but I also learned to obey better. Wherever and whenever He tells me to write, I write, being in the will of God (at least for that moment in time), not writing how and what I approve by my understanding, but His will through the voice of faith.

With faith and obedience comes growth and maturity, but this growth and maturity develop through what is known as trials; the Bible refers to it as sanctification, guiding us from naive faith to wisdom in Christ. However, this sanctification is not what we often assume in zeal as the perseverance of a perfect walk. It is shaped by conviction, a broken spirit, and a contrite heart—amidst falls from pride and sins, rescued by His grace. Through these trials, mistakes, mountaintop moments, and nights of the soul, we choose to surrender.

Ironically, there is victory in surrender—the same triumph found in trusting and letting go in faith despite life's circumstances telling us, "If I do not take matters into my own hands, then I will be at the mercy of the natural powers and influences that be." But "consider the ravens: They do not sow or reap; yet God feeds them. How much more valuable you are than the birds!" Luke 12:24. I discovered a somewhat paradoxical victory when I feel defeated by my failures and sins. God closed all doors before me, and through His provident love, often in my sin and shame, He led me to the end of myself. When I cry, "Father, help my unbelief, I believe you," I come to trust in His grace, receiving His sweet provision and rest, one day at a time, even amid doubt and anxiety. As a result, I have gained a new understanding, peace, and a renewing mind.

Proving the Will of God
The latter part of our primary scripture says.

...that ye may prove what (is) that good, and acceptable and perfect, will of God.

This tells us that it is not just an accomplishment, but something to be discovered, walked in, and perfected. It is not only what we do, but how and where we walk with Him. How can I get to that place in my life?

The word of God is effective; it says to "prove," and the insight of the Spirit finds the word "find" in my vocabulary. That is, you may find what is the good and right path. Once found, you must walk in an acceptable way—that is, according to God's standard. Finally, the text says, perfect—implying ongoing maturity and consistency. After discovering the good way and walking in it acceptably, you are then called to perfect that walk in harmony with God's righteousness (giving God preeminence in all things).

So again we ask, "How?" How do we arrive at that place?

The word that indicates the entrance to that path is "by," verse 2 tells us, "by the renewing of your mind" ...

Romans 12:2 says.
*And be not conformed to this world: But be ye transformed **by** the renewing of your mind...,*

But how do you renew your mind? To what end, and by what means?
Colossians 3:10 says.
And have put on the new (man), which is renewed in knowledge after the image of him that created him: ...But Christ is all in all (vs. 11).

So, to "what" are we renewed? To the image of God or the character of Christ. In the knowledge of God in His likeness. Note: this is not knowledge in the academic or religious sense. If it were, "being born again" could be by doctrine alone.

The scripture says, *"in knowledge after the image of him that created him,"* and 1 Corinthians 2:11 says,...*even so the things of God knoweth no man, but the Spirit of God.*

In other words, renew your mind in the spirit of the word. Paul expressed this in Ephesians 4:23: "And be renewed in the spirit of your mind." 1 Corinthians chapter two illustrates this concept. Verse 16 states: *"...for who hath known the mind of the Lord, that he may instruct him? But we have the mind of Christ."*

Our aim is the will of God, which you may interpret as a place of abode in God. However, perhaps the bigger question is, how do you get there? We see that the entrance is by renewing your mind in the spirit. Do not be misled; it is necessary to read, study, and understand the word academically. At the same time, it is more than that; it is not just the content of your mind, but the character and disposition of your mind, which brings us back to that foundational path, or gateway, which is a renewed mind.

Romans 12:1 says.

I beseech you therefore, brethren, by the mercies of God, that ye present your bodies a living sacrifice, holy, acceptable unto God, (which is) your reasonable service.

As you can see, we began with the scripture from the bottom up, and we are now at the midpoint, which states, "your reasonable service."

Where "how" questions the required means, this is the only time "how" requires any action on our part. Before we proceed, I must clarify that when I say this is the only time our action is required, I am merely stating a point in the perpetuation of the principle of God, working through the human vessel to fulfill the scripture. This scripture must be fulfilled continuously (in principle) to maintain this acceptable place in the Lord. When it is perfected, it may seem natural or effortless on your part; nevertheless, it continues.

So, what is our part or reasonable service?

The verse answers plainly, *"Present your bodies as a living sacrifice, holy, acceptable unto God."* Then, verse 2 follows: *"You should not conform, but be transformed."* Furthermore, verse 3 begins to explain how we begin presenting our bodies and minds for transformation.

Paul first places himself within this context to guide us on how we begin renewing our minds: "For by the grace given to me." Our proper service begins, not with outward actions or how we think about others, but by grace through faith.

Paul said, *"For by the grace given to me, I say to every one of you: Do not think of yourself more highly than you ought but rather think of yourself with sober judgment, in accordance with the faith God has distributed to each of you."* (Romans 12:3 NIV)

First, lower your sense of self-importance and self-created thoughts, and listen to what the gospel says about you. What is your faith, whether through mercy, conviction, faith, or revelation? Then move by grace. Do not be uplifted by your own standards; instead, soberly recognize that your importance comes from what has been given to you. And although it has been given to you, it is not based on your primary significance but on your participation in the body. As a member of the body, your function comes from the life shared throughout it, and the life of this body is the faith of Christ as imparted in the Church.

Often, with the young, anxiety arises from questions like: How do I know when to act in faith, or whether a certain inclination is the voice of faith? Is it measurable by the mandate Christ gives the Church? We sometimes get it wrong, but the body's unity sustains us at that stage, guiding us in our faith and emphasizing its presence. Once the anxiety subsides, we begin to understand the end of verse three: *"in accordance with the faith God has distributed unto you."* – You start aligning your thoughts with those of the body, in harmony, as you pursue a common goal with sober judgment.

Verses 4-6 explain that just as our body has different members and functions, we are all part of the One Body of Christ, each with various gifts. These gifts, given according to the grace of God, should be exercised by your faith (if your gift is prophesying, then prophesy according to the measure of grace of your faith). With the gift evident in you and the enablement of God's grace, you may exercise it accordingly. Verses 7 and 8 continue with the appropriate list: If service, serve; if teaching, be faithful in teaching; he who gives, give according to your faith, and so on.

Verses 9 to 21 explain why you should humble your thoughts, as stated in verse three, and outline the journey with its tensions, conflicts, and expectations. Without a humble view of yourself in your thinking and complete trust in God, you will not be able to do the following:

- *Let love be sincere (KJV says "without dissimulation") ...*
- *Never be lacking in zeal...*
- *Practice hospitality.*
- *Bless those who persecute you...*
- *Do not be conceited...*
- *Do not take revenge," It is mine to avenge; I will repay," says the lord.*
- *Do not be overcome by evil, but overcome evil with good.*

These are not just moral exhortations but the fruits of a renewing mind and a surrendered body. They do not come naturally to us; they are cultivated by the ongoing offering up of ourselves to God.

Yielding and the Grace of Meekness

Second, we should override our natural inclinations in response to natural circumstances with a spirit of meekness. Or should I say, our natural inclinations will be overridden by the grace given in the spirit of meekness.

Responding to or misinterpreting external circumstances is easy, which often leads us to act prematurely with good intentions but negative consequences. We perceive situations based on our fortunes, whether good or bad, and take actions aimed at personal correction and growth because, by nature, we are wired for self-preservation and self-promotion. However, even when considering our God-given good, our faith depends on the Body and should always reflect the faith of Christ, the Christ of Scripture. Things brought about in Christ are counted alive unto God. Everything else is dead and only benefits your members in futility, or dead works.

Romans 6:11 says; *Likewise, reckon also yourself to be dead indeed unto sin, but alive unto God through Jesus Christ our Lord.*

As Christ died on the cross as a sacrifice for sin and rose from the dead, so we also must die in Christ unto sin to live unto God and continue in holiness, which is acceptable unto God.

Romans 6:19 says, *"For as ye have yielded your members servants to uncleanness and to iniquity unto iniquity: even so now yield your members servants to righteousness unto holiness."*

If you look at this scripture properly, you will see that your part is not even in your power but instead in yielding yourself to the power of righteousness. However, you can still ask, how does this all get started?

To revise, verse 1 of the main text says, *"by the mercies of God."*

Romans 2:4 says, ... *despisest thou the riches of his goodness and forbearance and longsuffering; not knowing that the goodness of God leadeth thee to repentance?*

In repentance, we are baptized into the death of Christ through the mercies of God's expiation, so that we may be raised in the righteousness of God, and from that righteousness, we obey unto holiness. Repentance is at the beginning of every renewed mind. It stands on both sides of the track, in conviction as a sinner and sanctification as a saint, lowering your estimation of yourself and giving preeminence to the body. Even at this point, there remains a "how" because it extends across our salvific experience in various aspects. Let us first examine the top of the scripture, and then we may look at it from the outside.

"Therefore" — What It's There For

Romans 12 begins with, "I beseech you, therefore." I heard it said: whenever you see the word "therefore," especially at the beginning of a chapter, ask what it is there for. Moreover, this one follows an urgent plea (I beseech thee). Verse twenty in the previous chapter gives us the answer (Romans 11:20); it says,

"Well, because of unbelief, they were broken off, and thou stand by faith. Be not high-minded, but fear; for God spared not the natural branches, take heed lest he also spare not thee."

The key statement here is, "thou stand by faith." Paul is speaking to the unnatural branches, which we are: Gentiles. If so, then we must first be grafted into the natural olive tree of God's people before we can stand. This is the "how" that perpetuates from that very foundation of entering the will of God: salvation by faith.

Confession, Righteousness, and Salvation

Romans 10:9-10 says,

That if thou (the unsaved man) shalt confess with thy mouth the Lord Jesus and believe in thine heart that God has raised him from the dead, thou shalt be saved.

For with the heart man (any man) believeth unto righteousness; and with the mouth confession is made unto salvation.

These two verses may seem to repeat the same idea, but express two parts of a whole.

- Verse 9 explains how you enter into salvation: confess with your mouth... and believe in your heart, that Christ is risen. This results in justification - being made right with God.
- However, verse 10 explores the process further, ...for with the heart man believeth unto righteousness: belief produces righteousness. Here, the man is already justified. Nevertheless, confession remains the outward expression of inward faith that continues in our salvation (present continuous).

This is not merely justification, but what Reformed theology calls the perseverance or preservation of the saints. The last part of verse 10 tells us that the way you begin is the way you end, "confession of faith."

Romans 8:10 says,

"But what saith it? The word is nigh thee, (even) in thy mouth, and in thy heart: that is the word of faith, which we preach.)

The Perpetual "How" of Faith

So then the "how" as we continue in the will of God, extends across three aspects but stands on that pivotal statement of Paul, "Thou standest by faith."

They are,

1. Repentance in the conviction of the heart unto righteousness by the Word of Truth.
2. Humility, the sober judgment of oneself, lowering one's thoughts according to the faith God has measured to each.
3. Confession of faith, the outward expression of the inward belief, unto salvation.

These three work together in progression as we enter and walk in God's will.

However, even here we must acknowledge a mystery, because it is impossible to make an objective inquiry into the will of God without revelation. As creatures, we cannot perceive the fullness of the divine will. However, by special revelation, God has given us a perspective from eternity through His Prophets and Apostles, as seen in Paul's experience in the third heaven or John's on the Isle of Patmos.

One cannot stay within a thing and see its whole or even at a considerable close range. However, when you step back, what offers a clear distinction of the whole is its beginning and its end.

Salvation as God's Vision

I said all this to say concerning Romans 10:10 – "and with the mouth, confession is made unto salvation."

A theological description of "salvation" is this: Man's proper end, the attainment of the vision of God as in heaven. In other words, it is a holistic work seen from God's perspective, and to see that is to gain a bird's-eye view. Thus, you may say that the will of God is present in your life from the day you are saved until the day of your proper end. Our concern is walking in it by perpetuating the "how" and following a methodical blueprint as Scripture prescribes, which the Spirit illuminates. With a shared perspective of His bird's eye view, we will, by God's grace, navigate the corridors (the how) of salvation.

Chapter 4

Catechumen: Pursuing the truth

As we continue to broaden our perspective and pursue the "how" of our salvation, or the will of God, we will examine the aspects in which the "how" extends across our salvific experience. The first aspect states, Repentance in the conviction of the heart unto righteousness by the Word of truth. However, examining all three aligns with Christ's declaration, "I am the way, the truth, and the life." Again, he says, "My word is truth," in another place, he states, "The word that I speak to you is spirit and life." Thus, one of the broader perspectives along the way is the eyes of Truth or spiritual eyes, which enable us to walk in truth.

Moreover, I will give you a new heart and put a new spirit within you [for a new rationality; emotion, mind and will]; *and I will remove the heart of stone* [incapable of changing state of choice] *from your flesh and give you a heart of flesh* [malleable]. *I will put My Spirit within you and cause you to walk in My statutes* [for transformation], *and you will be careful* [choosing] *to observe My ordinances.* - Ezekiel 36:26,27

The conversion and discipleship of a man involves three aspects: (1) the regeneration of the human spirit; (2) the gift of the Holy Spirit with the ability to do His will; and (3) the sanctification of the soul with the heart's desire to do His will. The cause arises between "2" and "3". It is a transition between an acquired capacity and applied ability (the power of will), walking in His statutes (following His Word), and observing His ordinances, reflecting your daily choices.

This cause can be likened to resolving a conflict. At "2," you gain the ability to do His will, but less often the desire to do it. However, at "3," transformation occurs with the heart's new desires.

To differentiate by example:

*"But if any of you lacks **wisdom**, let him **ask** of God, who gives to all generously and without reproach, and it will be given to him."*

The statute is to "ask of God" or pray, in obedience to His Word by the efficacy of His Spirit—you pray, and He answers. Conversely, the ordinance embodies wisdom, subject to sanctification, maturity, and the exercise of the gifts He has given you to make the right choices in everyday life and practical living.

Man's cooperative role in salvation is demonstrated through baptism as a statute. This does not mean it is a choice of his will in conversion, as conversion is solely by the grace of God; rather, it is an act of obedience. This obedience continues throughout the believer's life through various forms of sanctification, allowing the redeemed will to choose what God has redeemed us for before the world. Yet, before we can genuinely demonstrate that choice, we must understand what our faith entails, which is the purpose of Catechumens: To learn His statutes to walk in them and observe His ordinances.

Catechumen: 1: a Christian convert receiving training in doctrine and discipline before baptism. 2: one receiving instruction in the fundamental doctrines of Christianity before admission to communicant membership in a church. -Webster

Katecheo: to sound down into the ear; i.e., (by implication) to indoctrinate, ("catechize") or (genitive) to apprise of: - inform, instruct, teach. – Strong's

The derivative words (kata and echos) suggest echo based on a distributive opposition that displaces or reverberates change.

The gospel is God's power to save all who believe; the catechumen is growing in that power to inform the will's agency toward faithfulness.

It serves as our agent of change in sanctification. Essentially, it represents discipleship from the infancy of faith to more informed growth in faith.

Agency is the <u>abstract</u> principle that "autonomous" beings or agents can act independently to make informed and voluntary decisions based on their <u>knowledge</u> and intention.

For example, two individuals in courtship will exercise the abstract principle of agency by using what they know about each other to make an informed decision about whether to marry as intended.

Baptism is the first genuine choice of a man's will or the initial exercise of human liberty after the will has been redeemed, informed by the new internal knowledge gained through an encounter with the Spirit of Christ. Therefore, Christ says, "whoever acknowledges me before others, I will also acknowledge him before my Father in Heaven," and vice versa. It represents our position in the cosmic struggle for the will that began in the garden. Adam never reflected on the choices of his will; he was cloaked in the glory of God's will; thus, he was unaware of his nakedness. A choice arose only with Satan's voice, as man (Adam) exercised his agency to follow a prompting outside the will of God (equating the ability to choose between two options), creating a choice between disobedience to or obedience to another. This is where Christ comes in; salvation in Jesus Christ is both the eternal redemption of humanity and the freedom of the agency of the will, but the security of that redemption can be found only in Christ. Man may stumble, but he always has the assurance of his redemption in Christ. However, man must stand in moral contrast with the world at pivotal moments in this sanctification. Baptism represents that initial stance. To illustrate this more clearly, consider the days of martyrdom, a form of ultimate baptism—there is no greater representation of the immersion of faith or of standing in contrast with the world. A public declaration of faith in Christ was for the brave and the newly willing, as such an action risked one's life and required standing against the world.

What does all this have to do with Catechumens?

The Catechumen is fundamentally a means of apostolic orthodoxy for discipleship, grounded in Romans 12:1-3 and Matthew 28:19,20. We must make disciples by teaching them to follow all that we were commanded and be transformed by a renewed mind. The Catechumen is a student of the Word who resists worldly influences and is sanctified throughout their journey according to God's will. However, its purpose in shaping the human will, which is inclined away from our natural tendencies by our redeemed state, diminishes when we trade our intellectual and moral responsibilities for a false grace of infused knowledge believed to arise at spiritual birth; or when it is treated as universal dogmatism through intellectual persuasion and moral law without spiritual conversion, rendering it ineffective at both extremes. In its living form, it is most beneficial after conversion to prepare for baptism; before this, it resembles preaching and can only serve as good news to the sinner, not as a delay of baptism. Conversely, for someone who has truly converted, even without the opportunity for baptism, the living efficacy of the word will providentially lead them to acknowledgment through sanctification in Christ. The Catechumenate is a continual process reserved for the regenerated, always learning, and guided by the Spirit of sanctification and grace. This sanctifying grace is found in the command to "share" between the student and the teacher.

"*And let the one who is* <u>*taught*</u> *the word* <u>*share*</u> *all good things with him who* <u>*teaches*</u>". – Galatians 6:6

This command signifies a fellowship, established through the contributions and benefits shared among parties in communion or congregation.

Catechism

Catechisms serve as effective vehicles of truth for individuals of any age, provided their contents are biblical and understandable truths, rather than being tailored to specific denominational beliefs or dogmas. Growing up in the Catholic Church, we recited the Apostles' Creed, which I knew as the "I Believe." These truths and other teachings shaped my worldview and provided a foundational platform for salvation; however, they should not have been regarded (as they were in my religious upbringing) as meritorious achievements, as they were during my communion and confirmation in Roman Catholicism.

As believers, we are expected to go well beyond the basics of Catechism to "study to show yourself approved." This pursuit is not merely about securing a rite of passage into fellowship, especially if you intend to take a non-concessive approach to the will of God while working out your own salvation. Paul explains in Hebrews 5 about this salvation, stating that if we want to understand these matters, we must become sharp in our hearing (vs. 11) to the extent that we are teachers (vs. 12). However, if we grow and learn to partake of the Holy Spirit, we can walk securely and rest in the confidence of our salvation, knowing we are sealed until the day of the Lord, as our senses are exercised to discern good and evil (vs. 14).

Therein lies the difference between religion and the will of God; some people refer to it as the difference between religion and a relationship. The truth is, even within religion, there can be a genuine relationship. Once there is a valid covenant, the difference lies in eternalizing an intrinsic affection for God or intimately aligning your life with Jesus. As a believer, I have come to realize that the zealous and passionate claims of brotherhood we often express in the body of Christ can sometimes devolve into mere religion. In the many congregations I have been a part of, we were taught to love our brethren, and rightly so. However, we received guidance through religious practices and sacrifice, which, in essence, tend to be performative. Although those practices and sacrifices are essential habits, they represent religious zeal, and we need to transcend that, going beyond the outward, cordial activities. We must reach a point where an internal bond compels us to seek reconciliation even when there is wrongdoing and offense in our actions.

We often discover that moving beyond religious sacrifices to genuine love, especially during separations, requires more than religious institutions to sustain relationships. This is not to say that relationships and religious fervor are invalid; they are essential for authentic fellowship, but religious fervor has its limits. Therefore, we cannot stop there. We must examine our faith to find ways to transition from zeal to love. Shift from a legalistic and ritualistic approach to intimate relationships, from a mechanical practice of the Bible to a faith defined by a deep affection for others. Since we are the house of faith, our intimacy must begin with faith and flow from the Father, and the intimacy of faith with the Father is prayer.

Chapter 5

Prayer

Then Jesus returned to the disciples and found them sleeping. "Were you not able to keep watch with me for one hour?" He asked Peter. "Watch and pray so that you will not enter into temptation. For the spirit is willing, but the body is weak." Matthew 26:40,41.

The scripture says, "Watch and pray," a state of living hope and active engagement. Prayer is not based on religious formulas, but rather on procedure. When the disciples asked Jesus to teach them how to pray, He said, "Do not keep on babbling like pagans... for your Father knows what you need before you ask Him."

He then gave them this model prayer, commonly known as the Lord's Prayer. The intriguing aspect of this prayer is that you can recite it as it is, which is sufficient to pray according to God's will and simple enough for our understanding and convictions. However, as you grow, this prayer also serves as a spiritual framework, simple enough for our recitation yet capable of guiding us through the revealed will of God by the Spirit.

"This then is how you should pray."

"Our Father in heaven, hallowed be your name."

Romans chapter eight testifies to our freedom in the Spirit of Christ, which delivers us from the sinful nature and the weakness of the law so that we can please God. It also states,

"For those who are led by the Spirit of God are the children of God. ...And by him, we cry 'Aba, Father.'

The Spirit himself testifies to our spirit that we are the children of God." (vs14-16).

"Your kingdom come, your will be done, on earth as it is in heaven."

Romans continues, "For the creation waits in eager expectation for the children of God to be revealed. ...That the creation itself will be liberated from its bondage to decay and brought to the freedom and glory of the children of God" (vs. 19-22)

Creation itself is linked to our redemption and glory, but it follows the preordained will of God in heaven.

"Give us today our daily bread. And forgive us our debts, as we also have forgiven our debtors."

Hebrews chapter three begins by reminding us as "partakers of the heavenly calling, consider the Apostle and High Priest of our profession," some translations say confession. It warns us not to harden our hearts, as the Israelites did in the wilderness due to their unbelief, which prevented them from entering His rest. Chapter four continues with the same theme, "for there is still left a rest to be entered in by faith." (vs 3). So yes, if we are to rest, our work is finished, and we should look to Him for our daily provision. However, since we cannot pay our debts through work, He has forgiven us. Likewise, he expects us to forgive those who owe us.

"And lead us not into temptation but deliver us from the evil one."

Chapter four of Hebrews concludes by emphasizing Jesus as our great high priest, and consequently, we should hold fast to our profession/confession.

"For we have not a high priest which cannot be touched with the feeling of our infirmities; but was in all points tempted like as we are, yet without sin." (Vs. 15).

He understands our feelings and has endured the temptations, "yet without sin," so He can deliver us from the evil one. Considering all this, the last verse of chapter four states,

"Let us therefore come boldly unto the throne of grace, that we may obtain mercy, and find grace to help in time of need." (Vs 16)

We come to the Father in confidence, knowing that we are welcome. And not just welcome but carried along in grace by real help. Hebrews 1:14, speaking of the angels, says,

"Are they not all ministering spirits, sent forth to minister for them who shall be heirs of salvation?"

Vigil in Prayer

The spirit of man is willing, but his flesh is weak. So what keeps us persevering through our natural weaknesses to stay faithful and resist temptations, to stay awake and keep watch for an hour?

Now in the same way the Spirit also helps our weakness; for we do not know what to pray for as we should, but the Spirit Himself intercedes for us with groanings too deep for words; and He who searches the hearts knows what the mind of the Spirit is, because He intercedes for the saints according to the will of God. (Romans 8:26,27)

When Jesus taught his disciples to pray, he advised them not to keep babbling with many words, for God already knows what we need. Yet, in the Garden, he asks them, *"Can't you watch with me one hour?...and pray that you do not fall into temptation."* An hour is a long time to pray. After five minutes, most people typically start to repeat themselves and, after a bit longer, begin to nod off. However, there is a type of prayer that can keep you bright-eyed and engaged, with genuine fervor, throughout the night. It is the vigil prayer.

Prayer is also a vigil of faith; it is a way to remain in the manifested presence of God. I cannot lie; I have not grasped its full implications, but from my experience, its importance has not escaped me. The Holy Spirit woke me on seasonal occasions, sometimes between one and four a.m., impressing specific things upon my spirit, even those far from my immediate concern. I remember back in 2004 when I had an urgent need to pray for the victims of child sexual trafficking and abuse while in Grenada, and often for fellow believers and issues close to home. But sometimes we are meant to stay reverently in His presence during those times. Some more mature Saints can attest to this as a regular occurrence, where the Holy Spirit summons and carries you in prayer. God does not desire many words or long prayers because our soul's desires naturally drive us, or we do not know how to pray. We come to Him in our time of need and confess His will through recitation, but by His Spirit, He urges us to be vigilant. Praying for an hour against the pressure of sleep (when you are usually asleep) is almost impossibly challenging. Yet, we ought to be diligent in our pursuit, and God will make us vigilant in His presence. It does not end when we go back to sleep at 4:30 AM, but continues in a state of mindfulness as we go about our day, diligent in our pursuits, shielded by His provision and His will. So, in essence, prayer is the power of God's will.

We often think of prayer as an upload, where we present our will and desires to persuade God, but in truth, it is the opposite; it's more like a download. In prayer, we align with God's will, saying, "Not our will but your will be done," and "Be transformed by the renewing of our mind."

We often hold a vigil as a religious practice to accompany our spiritual endeavors and missionary work, which is good. However, I'm afraid we tend to use prayer merely to support our work in hopes of ensuring success, aligning with some interpretations of James' "faith without works is dead."

True prayer embodies its works and power; some translations call it "fervent prayer." Even James states, "The prayer of a righteous person is powerful and effective," citing Elijah's prayer, "that it will not rain, and it did not rain for three and a half years. And again, he prayed, and the heavens gave rain." (Vs. 16-18). This also points to the effectiveness of prayer within our fellowship, where we confess our sins and pray for one another so that we may be healed, of which I can personally testify.

In 2008, I lived in Boca Raton, FL, with my cousin, Dave, for a while. I found a job and became a member of my cousin's friend's church in Boynton Beach while I was in Florida. During that time, I developed what seemed to be a skin fungus that spread across the right side of my face. It became more noticeable and worsened no matter what I did. But I remember one night reading James, and suddenly, this scripture came alive to me:

Is anyone among you sick? Let them call the elders of the church to pray over them and anoint them with oil in the name of the Lord. And the prayer offered in faith will make the sick person well.

Right then and there, I knew my face would heal if I followed what this scripture said. It wasn't just a general declaration of faith or scripture about believing in the word. No. At that moment, during prayer and meditation behind closed doors, something came alive in the text and was implanted in my spirit, granting me the faith to heal my face. I recognized it right then and there. I eagerly awaited Bible study the following evening to share this text, which felt different from all the other times I read it, and said to Pastor Devon, "Look! The scripture says if you anoint me with oil and pray, I will be healed," and that I did. If memory serves correctly, I believe it was a Wednesday evening. In the meantime, until Sunday, I was skeptical, thinking I only saw improvements because that's what I wanted to see. But as soon as I entered the sanctuary, everyone who was present during our prayer of faith became excited. "It's healing!" They noticed the difference right away. And as they say, the rest is history. As the week went on, I stopped wearing my hat to cover the rash on my face, which cleared up quickly without any treatment.

Prayer is rooted in two frameworks of the Christian walk: the legal and the relational. It is vital to the structure of the believer's life, serving as the nucleus of faith and a necessary engagement for a successful journey, inextricably linked to faith and obedience. At times, it involves simply exercising your faith, while at other times, it is a response in obedience to that faith. Furthermore, prayer can serve as the discerning factor between your motives and affections in pursuing your desires and ambitions; at other times, it expresses your grief and petitions. Just as the Spirit assists us in every other aspect of our Christian walk, He also supports us in our weakness when it comes to prayer.

Solomon said, "The fear of the Lord is the beginning of wisdom," but how do you begin in that wisdom? It's through prayer, in the asking. Even Solomon's wisdom was a response to a prayer. James 1:5 says, "If any man lacks wisdom, let him ask of God, who gives generously to all without reproach, and it will be given him." But it doesn't end there; the following verse states, "But let him ask in faith, with no doubting, for the one who doubts is like a wave of the sea that is driven and tossed by the wind." Some translations say, "nothing wavering." So yes, there is the initial assurance, and a trusting approach by faith, but also a relational abiding, not being "driven and tossed by the wind." James 1:9 says, "Believers in humble circumstances ought to take pride in their high position." That's abiding faith—actively engaging on earth in prayer and trusting in God and, by extension, being positioned high in the arms of God. In the next verse, the rich are to take pride in their humiliation. What humiliation? What is more humiliating than for the rich to get on their knees?

Most of the time, prayer is not for the return of an answer, but for the solution to our anguish and daily anxiety, which has become all too common in the world and within the body of Christ. But as believers, we can "Consider it all joy...when we encounter various trials" because we know it is to prove the trustworthiness of our faith, and that proof is to produce endurance in us, "so that you may be mature and complete, not lacking anything."

This brings us back to verse 5, "If any of you lack wisdom, you should ask   God." Prayer serves as the spiritual protection and shield of our being, the offense of the Spirit, and the means of receiving guidance from above. It reflects the nature of an intimate and comforting relationship.

Prayer, like communication between individuals, shapes and reflects the essence of our relationship with God. We grow closer through vulnerability and affection, establishing boundaries through love and respect rather than laws and fear. Prayer serves as a means of internal communication, while the law entails external and restricted interaction. However, if you limit or disregard this privilege, your relationship begins to resemble your connection with outsiders or the law. Neglected relationships, similar to a household grappling with unresolved issues and minimal communication, can foster tension since they lack the outsider's freedom to walk away. Like our natural relationships, our words are not always sufficient to convey our feelings. Sometimes, less is more; we may remain silent even during active communication, responding only when prompted. At other times, we cling to the essence of our last interaction, feeling as if we cannot break through or that there is a lack of response, yet our love and essential communication remain intact. In prayer, we persevere without ceasing.

Occasionally, the issue lies within our hearts, stemming from a lack of desire or yearning for something else. Naturally, we strive to overcome these feelings and navigate them as best we can, but God does not forsake us. Yes, we may find ourselves in that quiet place, yet even when we feel unheard, we continue to exercise our faith, consciously acknowledging our state. While we may lack the ability to "restore" communication, we do possess the power to turn or repent.

As you initially approached the Sovereign God, the same method of prayer is necessary to maintain that relationship. At first, the issue was with our hearts, and once the conviction of faith emerged, we cried, "Lord, save me!" Thus, you restore the heart by reaffirming the confession of faith. As discussed in the chapter "Quested by Anxiety," we addressed the "how" that arises from our salvific experience in which the will of God is revealed:

For with the heart, a man believes unto righteousness, and with the mouth, confession is made unto salvation ('the attaining of Man's proper end').

Romans 12:1 speaks of our reasonable service, and I noted that this is the only instance where "how" requires any action on our part as part of the ongoing principle of God. Therefore, we continue our salvific walk, "...and with the mouth, confession is made unto salvation," remaining in the present continuous tense. We also offer prayer as a living sacrifice to God as part of "our reasonable service." However, even when it goes beyond our reasonable service, Christ intercedes on our behalf. This underscores how vital prayer is to our journey; it is the lifeline of our spiritual existence.

The gravity of Prayer - A response to spiritual gravity.

We recognize and acknowledge that, by the force of gravity, we remain grounded. A toddler reaches out to avoid falling during his first attempt to walk, but the parents do not reach out to catch him. He must learn to balance between the same gravity that causes him to fall. Thus, our prayers often do not yield immediate responses or results to our requests or expectations of God. Nevertheless, prayer and the apparent lack of response are necessary for our development.

The same gravity that keeps us safely on the ground, often without our realizing its power, must now be respected as a boundary that anchors a structure for scaling height, where a misstep could lead to disaster. Therefore, prayer is a sacred realm that deserves respect. It has the power to move mountains, while divination can lead to a curse.

With excellent engineering, an aircraft can take off from one landmass and land safely on another, guided by gravity. However, this is possible only if we first understand the environmental laws at work. Thus, prayer is just one component of a spiritual environment.

Unlike gravity, where engineering can manipulate elements for desired outcomes, we should not attempt to manipulate prayer through religious formulas. We obey the law and trust in its efficacy. Our efforts come through faith by grace, and the Sovereign hand of God will carry out His will.

The relational efficacy of prayer is not maintained by its asking aspect, but by its abiding nature. You can ask of a Sovereign God, but you abide in a loving Father. Still, both actions can serve as the same outreach; you may approach a Sovereign God or a loving Father while abiding in Him. You pray to the Sovereign God and dwell in the Father's love, while Christ ensures the continued relationship. It is in Christ you pray, and in Christ you abide. Christ established His church to prevail against hell and gave us legal access to the Kingdom of God. *"... I will build My church, and the gates of Hades will not prevail against it. I will give you the keys of the kingdom of heaven, and whatever you bind on earth will be bound in heaven, and whatever you loose on earth will be loosed in heaven."*

As stated in the previous chapters, young believers are often driven by anxiety. As we renew our minds, we exercise sober judgment and acknowledge our limited perspective. We learn that truth is the open door through which we broaden our understanding by walking in His statutes as students of the Word and genuine catechumens, informing our will to faithfulness. As we mature, our expectations extend beyond the rudiments of catechism; we ought to study to show ourselves approved, becoming sharp in our discernment to the point of becoming teachers who better understand our salvation. As we continue to grow, we mature as partakers of the Holy Spirit, becoming better able to discern between good and evil, and gaining sharper spiritual vision for a broader understanding of God's will.

Chapter 6

A Bird's-Eye View

From previous chapters, we examine the believer's walk as they pursue the Will of God and determine that, in truth, knowing God's will is seeing it from His perspective as a distinctive whole, that is, His will on earth. We often begin to seek the will of God for our individual lives; however, we usually fail to consider two key things. We are in God only as far as we are in Christ, and in Christ as far as His Church. We know that our salvation is in Christ, who is and was the exact representation of the Father on earth. But now, as He is no longer in the world in the flesh, He has given His Church as His body. Thus, the Church is now His representation on earth. We must also acknowledge that this whole we seek reflects a greater Will purposed in eternity, and this reflection is now the Church. What we need to ask now is, what is God's will for the Church?

Now, you may ask, why is it necessary to know the will of the Church, and what does that have to do with the will of God for your life? First, a man's Will is his inheritance, or rather, who inherits his estate or kingdom. A man can have only one valid will; likewise, there is one inheritance in the will of God, which is His Church accomplished in Christ.

As we began exploring the scriptures in chapter one, Romans 12 presents a mindset prerequisite for transformation and a new worldview. It is somewhat similar to what the Exodus, Laws, and Prophets did in shaping the Hebrews into the nation of Israel. However, in this case, the new Israel of God is already here. As Christ said, "The Kingdom of Heaven is at hand," and the repatriation is occurring one soul at a time. Our purpose or inheritance in that kingdom is found in the Church, the body of Christ. Am I suggesting that the Church provides us with a bird's-eye view? Yes! And we will see this as the book progresses. Secondly, if we want to understand God's will from His point of view, we must be given an eternal perspective, which He possesses. Our most relevant example, other than Jesus, is Paul.

Listen to what he said in *2 Corinthians 12:1, 2.*

I will go on to visions and revelations of the Lord. I know a man in Christ who fourteen years ago-whether in the body I do not know, or out of the body I do not know, God knows - such a man was caught up to the third heaven.

And Acts 22:17-18 says, ...I was in a trance; and saw him saying unto me...

The word "trance" describes a state where the soul appears to have left the body or a state of rapture. This aligns with what Paul says in 2 Corinthians 12, Vs 1: "Whether in the body, I cannot tell...and vs. 4; ...and heard unspeakable words, which is not lawful for a man to utter." Paul neither read about it nor heard it; he experienced it. On his return, the mortal man was not allowed to express certain things. Part of my argument here is that I can somewhat relate to this.

In 2004, around the same time I began writing seriously, I lived in St. George, Grenada. I was studying Genesis Chapter One, and as I read the text, it became increasingly clear that there was more to learn, prompting me to start over and over again from the beginning to grasp what I had missed. However, there was that one instance; I was in a season of fasting and prayer, and as I reviewed the first two verses of chapter one once again, I do not remember how long it lasted, but in verse 2, it felt as though I was placed on pause. I experienced a physical prompting on the left side of my brain in the form of that pleasurable pain, except this time, it lasted throughout the experience. My mind was drawn into the text, as if pulled into the creation experience. I witnessed a segment, or glimpse, of creation and that stage's state or form. I am unsure if I can use the word 'stage' in this context. However, I remember a distinct revelation concerning time as it relates to eternity through the text at the end of verse 2 - "And the Spirit of God moved upon the face of the waters" - the Waters are the axis of time, which globed in-existence in existence (a piece of void was created within the eternal existence of God, axis(ed) on time and the foundation of water through which He formed our natural existence). I say in-existence because time is a line or bridge drawn across a void or a hole in eternity, and God sent His word and filled it; that is why there is a necessity for physical matter to couple with the Word for the manifestation of the supernatural. I saw it, but since then, I have not been able to form a complete mental picture because I lack a physical context to reference. Nevertheless, I saw it. Much of the text that previously seemed unable to explain creation now makes sense, not that it offers a complete explanation in English or our natural vernacular. Still, it makes sense because human languages cannot fully express it, nor can it be fully expressed in our understanding.

I was eager to return to the flesh to write down everything I observed. Subsequently, I picked up the pen and recalled what I had seen, but when I put the pen to paper, although it was in my mind, I could not translate it. Then the Holy Spirit said, "What is understood is written so that what cannot be written may be understood."

The fact is that Paul stepped into eternity to receive this mystery from a bird's-eye view, a type of rapture preview. He could not tell the difference from his natural body; he said God knew.

And what was the result of that trip?

Ephesians 3:3 says:

How that by revelation he made known unto me the mystery.

"The mystery!" Not, "A," mystery; the one thing purposed in time and eternity. How do we know that? Ephesians 3:9 cannot be clearer, and the New Living Translation is right on point; it says:

I was chosen to explain to everyone this plan that God, the creator of all things, had kept secret from the beginning.

This is the purpose of the Church: to manifest and fulfill God's will in time. King James calls it "the fellowship of the mystery." Consider the honor God has given to humanity; even the angels should look towards the Church to see the extent of God's wisdom.

Ephesians 3:10 continues:

To the intent that now unto the principalities and powers in heavenly (places) might be known by the Church the manifold wisdom of God, according to the eternal purpose which he purposed in Christ Jesus our Lord.

However, before we examine it from the Church's perspective as the inheritor of God's will, we must first consider it from the individual's point of view. Few believers seem to relate to expounded revelations or believe in an outer-world experience, such as I testified above. Mine is unique to me, and Paul's being caught up to "the third" heaven was unique to his call and apostleship. However, I am not special, and such an experience, along with the power that enables it, is not strange or abnormal to the believer, or at least it should not be. Remember, James, speaking to us about the power of prayer, referred to Elijah shutting up the heavens to rain, an example from the Old Testament. John the Baptist came in the spirit of Elijah as the forerunner of Jesus; speaking of him, Jesus said, "Even the least person in the kingdom of God is greater than he is."

What makes the least of us greater than John the Baptist?

What did Jesus say to Nicodemus?

"Except a man is born again (from above), he cannot enter the Kingdom of God."

Romans 8:9 says, *"You, however, are not in the realm of the flesh but are in the realm of the Spirit, if indeed the Spirit of God lives in you. And if anyone does not have the Spirit of Christ, they do not belong to Christ."*

So, we may not have a whole intellectual grasp of what is seen from above, but we have an intelligent grid of reference for God's perspective in Christ and a revelatory disclosure by the Spirit that dwells within us.

This makes the least of us in the Kingdom greater than all the saints of the Old Testament.

"What no eye has seen, what no ear has heard,
and what no human mind has conceived" —
the things God has prepared for those who love him—
these are the things God has revealed to us by his Spirit.
– 1 Corinthians 2:9-10.

In a sense, Paul's experience is not entirely unique. He is a pioneer of the Kingdom, but the mystery was given to all the saints and shared among the mature. Who are those who are mature? They are those within the Church, revealed to us by His Spirit through gifts:

And He gave some as apostles, some as prophets, some as evangelists, some as pastors and teachers, for the equipping of the saints for the work of ministry, for the building up of the body of Christ; until we all attain to the unity of the faith, and of the knowledge of the Son of God, to a mature man, to the measure of the stature which belongs to the fullness of Christ. -Ephesians 4:11-13.

Earlier, I stated how relatively few believers can relate to the supernatural through revelations, as they define our salvation. I believe that outer-world experiences can be part of our Christian walk. Those of us who testify to such experiences are not strange or special, nor is the power that enables those experiences abnormal for believers. Instead, there is an expectation of the promises of God and His Christ. I also spoke of my trance-like experience, where my mind was drawn into the text of Genesis 1:2. I have been reluctant to discuss this experience; frankly, I have not spoken of it in detail to anyone except in my writing. As I mentioned elsewhere, during my initial conversion and the first three years as a believer, my life was inundated with the voice and experience of the Holy Spirit. I recall trying to confide in close believers who claimed to have been in the faith for over thirty years, thinking that someone familiar with the Spirit and the things of God would be able to offer me some counsel, but it was the opposite. They looked at me oddly; one of the responses was, "Were you smoking that day?" or something to that effect. Ironically, my deliverance from dependence on marijuana is part of that testimony.

To give a quick recap on the voice of the Holy Spirit. People often refer to the voice of God with some ambiguity, meaning that hearing and obedience depend on a certain level of distinctiveness and a leap of faith. However, it is much more than that. Most of my experiences with the voice of the Holy Spirit were quite distinctive and shockingly recognizable the first time I heard it. I still ponder, "How was I able to recognize a voice with such clarity that I had not heard before?" I fell to the floor that first day, hands to my face in tears in response to the statement, "This is you." The voice came after reading Romans chapter one, which contains a slew of descriptions for the reprobates in the last five verses of the chapter. At the very end, the voice said, "This is you." That day, my repentance was a bit strange, as though lost in grief, as I cried out to God, 'Why did you allow me to become that way? Why didn't you stop me?'

I saw everything for the first time after getting up from that floor. I went outside, staring at the trees and the sky, amazed at God's creation. Then the voice came again, "You are enslaved," and I asked, "Enslaved by what?" "Enslaved by marijuana," followed by, "Go say this prayer, ..." He gave me a prayer to say word for word, and the rest is history.

There are other examples, such as when God led me to discover that the Spirit that suddenly indwells me has been present in millions of people. He told me, "Go over to your sister's house," then "turn on the television," to introduce me to Christian television. It is funny; I was a little mad then, saying, "How come nobody told me about this all this time?" Or the Holy Spirit telling me to go in and speak to my old stepfather, who was sick. That time, I disobeyed and said I would do it next time, tragically learning the next day why it was so important to speak to him then and there; he died the next day.

As I mentioned, the emphasis is on the voice of the Holy Spirit. The point is that He is a relevant and necessary companion who will be both new and familiar, much like recognizing the voice of a loved one, such as hearing your mother's or father's voice. However, in this case, He speaks from within you, not from you, and is distinctly recognizable apart from your internal thoughts and emotions; otherwise, He is self-originating and authoritative.

Now, I do not mean to dismiss the voice of ambiguity and the intuitive step of faith that many relate to when following God's voice; I believe this is also valid and may sometimes be necessary. However, I think those who rely solely on this to hear God's voice have missed out on primary communication experiences with the Holy Spirit. It is sort of like the children of Israel when God told them to sanctify themselves and come to speak to Him at the foot of the mountain, and they drew back in fear at the thunder and lightning and trumpet and smoke of the mountain and said to Moses, *"Speak to us yourself and we will listen. But do not have God speak to us, or we will die."*

We often struggle to hear the Holy Spirit amid the noise of an unsanctified soul. Yet, God needs to speak to us nonetheless, so He communicates through whatever measure of our faculties. Whether by our emotions, mind, or body, through prompting, conviction, or a sense of peace, He guides us in His will and presence. During my formative years as a believer, and to a lesser extent even today, I experienced a unique prompting used by the Holy Spirit, which initially helped me overcome my fear of spiders, among many other influences and communications. It is these actual pain-like sensations on both sides of my brain – on the right, an unpleasant, anguishing sensation indicating something bad, signaling to stop or change the course of action, or a heads-up about something undesirable; and a certain tension on the left side, which I refer to as pleasurable pain, suggesting that something good is happening, encouraging me to make this choice or indicating I am on the right track. Depending on the circumstances, the meaning is sometimes clear, but other times, I remain clueless until I discover what is hidden from me.

God also uses various ways to communicate with us, such as a profound peace that resonates with your soul, scripture, or even challenges and trials. However, one thing is clear: to be an effective Christian, the voice of God (anchored in His Word) must be prominent in our lives, and as believers, the Holy Spirit must be active within us.

In Peter's first sermon, God made it clear that this was to be expected, saying, "...this is what was spoken by the prophet Joel:"

'In the last days, God says, I will pour out my Spirit on all people.

Your sons and daughters will prophesy, your young men will see visions, your old men will dream dreams.

Even on my servants, both men and women, I will pour out my Spirit in those days, and they will prophesy.

I will show wonders in the heavens above and signs on the earth below, blood and fire and billows of smoke.

The sun will be turned to darkness and the moon to blood before the coming of the great and glorious day of the Lord.

And everyone who calls on the name of the Lord will be saved.' ..."

Acts 2:16-21.

And when the people, convicted, responded, *"'Brothers, what shall we do?'*

Peter replied, Repent and be baptized, every one of you, in the name of Jesus Christ for the forgiveness of your sins. And you will receive the gift of the Holy Spirit. The promise is for you and your children and for all who are far off—for all whom the Lord our God will call." - Acts 2:37-39.

This was at the inception of the Church when it was still a local, universal body; however, the Holy Spirit was prevalent, and there was a promise of active participation for all, "for you and your children and for all who are far off—for all whom the Lord our God will call."

So, yes, as individuals, we can ask, 'What is God's will for our lives?' However, if we are genuinely asking this question, you should already be there; you cannot effectively pose this question if you are not yet there; "No one can say 'Jesus is Lord' except by the Holy Spirit." Therefore, from an individual perspective, His will is that you repent, be baptized, and be filled with the Holy Spirit; afterward, you should consider what His will is for the Church.

With all this, we must conclude that we can no longer say, "The will of God for my life," but rather, "my life in the will of God," and consequently, consider our place in the Church along with the knowledge of the Church and its work.

And so, as part of any Body or institution, I have identified seven fundamentals we must grasp:

1. We must know its mission and purpose (**The Commission of the Church**). (Matthew 28:18-20).

2. We need to know by which principles and methods it operates. (**The functioning of the Church**). (Ephesians 3:8-11, 1 Corinthians 12:1-7).

3. I need to know where I fit in the scheme of things (**Our function in the Church**). (2 Peter 1:1-11).

4. I must know what is required of me and how to execute those duties (**Knowing and executing your duty**) (Romans 12:3-6).

5. We need to understand the order or line of authority by which the body operates and our place within that order. (1 Peter 2:5).

6. We need to yield to the Order sacrificially. (Luke 22:7, 41).

7. We need to yield in adequate proportion to our required service in duty and responsibility. (1 Corinthians 14:32, 33).

Chapter 7

The Commission of the Church

The Church has a twofold mission, established and demonstrated by Christ Himself, representing God's saving rule over His people on earth. This mission involves preaching the gospel to all nations, awakening the elect to their inheritance of eternal life. While the Church operates as a visible, tangible organization, its core inheritance is spiritual, eternal, and presently unseen, fulfilling the prayer, "Your kingdom come on earth as it is in heaven."

In scripture, there are four components of a biblical commission that every divine calling includes. They are:

I.   The authority by whom it is given - by God or Christ directly, which is the foundation; without it, there is no true commission.

II. The mission, which clarifies what the one commissioned is to do.

III. Empowerment, equipping the person to fulfill the mission.

IV. And accountability ensures they stay faithful to God's call.

It is never merely a suggestion; it is a charge given under God's authority, carried out through His enablement, and accountable only to Him.

The Great Commission, as outlined in Matthew 28:18-20, clearly states and encompasses everything that has been foreshadowed in every biblical mission. The Church fulfills this mission through Christ and in Him. In this commission, Christ gave a twofold mandate that shapes His body, the Church:

1. **Growth from without** – bringing in new disciples through evangelism and baptism.
2. **Growth from within** – forming disciples in obedience to His commands.

This twofold structure is the cycle of growth through which the kingdom of God on earth is built and the Church is maintained. Christ Himself first exemplified it, as the Church being His body, with the cycle beginning in Him, before He commanded His disciples to go into all the world and do the same.

Before His ascension, Jesus issued this final command to His disciples, instructing them to wait in Jerusalem for the promised gift of the Father, the Holy Spirit, or "power from above." The fulfillment of this promise at Pentecost marked the official inauguration of the Church, and with it, the Great Commission was set in motion. After Christ rose, the doors of the Church officially opened to the world at Pentecost, when the Spirit descended and the apostles carried out this commission for the first time in history. I recently heard the late Dr. Sproul say that he believes the Church officially started at the Last Supper in the upper room. I wouldn't dispute that.

The bible described the first cycle of this mission, which was accomplished in Christ beforehand (the Church being his body), as follows:

Though he were a Son, yet learned he obedience by the things which he suffered; And being made perfect, he became the author of eternal salvation unto all them that obey him; Called of God a high priest after the order of Melchisedec. - Hebrews 5:8-9

In this case, the authority by which he came was a Son. His mission was to suffer as a sacrifice, but he also exemplified our mission by making disciples and establishing them as pillars of the Church as apostles. He was made perfect and empowered as the author of our eternal salvation, to all who believe, and remains faithful as our high priest.

And Jesus came and spoke to them, saying, "All power is given unto me in heaven and in earth. Go ye therefore, and teach all nations, baptizing them in the name of the Father, and of the Son, and of the Holy Spirit: Teaching them to observe all things whatsoever I have commanded you: and, lo, I am with you always, even unto the end of the world. Amen." (Matthew 28:18-20)

(I)   The Authority of the Commission (Matthew 28:18)

Before giving any instruction, Jesus declared: *"All power* [authority] *is given unto me in heaven and in earth."* This statement affirms that the risen Christ has universal and eternal authority in both the heavenly realm and the created world.

The Church is founded solely on this authority, which is also the basis for the Great Commission. This commission is not the result of human planning, nor does it rely on social influence or clever strategies. When Christ instructed His apostles to wait in Jerusalem for *"the Promise of the Father"* (Acts 1:4), He ensured that the commission would be fulfilled not through human strength but by the power of the Spirit, acting under His authority.

Without that authority, commission is impossible, because without the Spirit, it is powerless in practice.

(II)   The mission has two objectives:

The **first Objective** is the Growth from Without (Matthew 28:19)

"Go ye therefore, and teach [make disciples of] *all nations, baptizing them in the name of the Father, and of the Son, and of the Holy Spirit."*

This first command is outward-facing. It is the call to go beyond the boundaries of the familiar, to reach all nations with the gospel, and to initiate them into the covenant through baptism.

The first fulfillment of this came at Pentecost (Acts 2:5–41). Godly Jews from every nation were gathered in Jerusalem when the Spirit descended, and they each heard the apostles speaking in their own languages. Peter stood and proclaimed Christ from the Law and the Prophets, bearing witness by the Holy Spirit to the crucified and risen Lord. The message pierced their hearts, and they cried out, *"Men and brethren, what shall we do?"* Peter replied, *"Repent, and be baptized every one of you in the name of Jesus Christ for the remission of sins, and ye shall receive the gift of the Holy Ghost."*

That day, about three thousand souls were added to the Church. Here is the outward movement of the commission: by the Spirit's power, the gospel is preached, heard, and received, and new believers are brought into the kingdom.

The **second Objective** is the Growth from Within (Matthew 28:20)

"Teaching them to observe all things whatsoever I have commanded you."

The second part of the commission shifts inward. It is not enough to bring people into the Church; they must be taught to live in obedience to all that Christ commanded. Notice the wording—it is not just "teach them what I commanded," but "teach them to observe." This suggests instruction, demonstration, and the development of habits of obedience.

Acts 2:42 illustrates this well: *"And they continued steadfastly in the apostles' doctrine and fellowship, and in breaking of bread, and in prayers."* This was not occasional activity but consistent devotion. Doctrine kept them grounded in truth; fellowship united them in love; the breaking of bread (the Lord's Supper) reminded them of Christ's sacrifice; and prayer linked them to God and each other.

Here, I must confess a personal belief. For years, I viewed communion as an optional regular practice. But according to Scripture, it is a command to remain steadfast in it, along with prayer, fellowship, and study. The inward growth of the Church is inseparable from these practices.

This inward focus also protects apostolic doctrine. The collection of commands given by Christ is complete, and the apostolic teaching creates a fixed standard by which all doctrine is evaluated. Any doctrine or practice must align with what has been handed down. This is the essence of apostolicity—it maintains the Church's purity and unity.

(III)   Empowerment for the Commission (Matthew 28:20; Acts 2:1–4)

Christ ends the commission with the promise: *"...and lo, I am with you always, even unto the end of the world."* His presence is not abstract—it is made real through the Holy Spirit poured out at Pentecost.

On that day, the Spirit filled the apostles, empowering them to speak with boldness and clarity in languages they had never learned. The gospel came with power, not just in words. Without this empowerment, evangelism becomes mere marketing, and discipleship turns into moral teaching without life. With the Spirit, both are infused with divine power and presence.

(IV)   Accountability in the Commission

The Great Commission is given *"unto the end of the age."* The Church in every generation is answerable for its faithfulness to this mission. The apostles, as the first witnesses, set the doctrinal and practical boundaries, and we are called to walk in them.

Faithfulness is measured not by innovation or cultural adaptation but by obedience—continuing to make disciples and teach them to observe Christ's commands, in both the outward and inward dimensions of the Church's life.

The Cycle of the Church's Mission

The twofold commission forms a living cycle, pivoting on Christ, the Apostles, and Pentecost by the outpouring of His Spirit to: **New**

Believers → Apostolic Teaching → Mature Disciples → New Evangelism → Repeat.

Break either part—evangelism without discipleship, or discipleship without evangelism—and the Church's witness is distorted. However, when both work together, the body grows in both number and maturity, fulfilling its calling in the world.

Faithfulness to the Twofold Commission

The Great Commission is not merely the Church's task; it is its lifeblood. Christ's authority undergirds it, His Spirit empowers it, and His presence sustains it. Pentecost shows us how it works in practice—growth from without through Spirit-empowered proclamation, and growth from within through steadfast devotion to apostolic teaching, fellowship, communion, and prayer.

To neglect either is to disobey Christ. To embrace both is to walk in the rhythm of the kingdom, knowing that He is with us always, even unto the end of the world. Amen.

EXAMPLES OF BIBLICAL COMMISSIONS

Examples	Authority	Mission	Empowerment	Accountability
Adam	God	Tend and keep the garden	Dominion over the earth	Obedience to God's Word
Noah	God	Build the ark and save his family	Instructions, favor	Covenant faithfulness
Moses	God (burning bush)	Led Israel from Egypt to the promised land	Signs, the staff, and God's presence	Obedience to the Law
Joshua	God	Lead Israel into Canaan	God's promise, law	Keeping covenant
Prophets	God	Call Israel to repentance	Word of the Lord	Faithful in message
Apostles	Christ	Make disciples of all nations	Holy Spirit and spiritual gifts	Faithful to the gospel

Chapter 8

The Functioning of the Church

Faith and Obedience

The functioning of the Church rests on two basic principles: faith and obedience, culminating in the mystery of love. These principles form the spiritual backbone of the Church's existence and operation. Every legitimate function of the Body, whether administrative, liturgical, or missional, finds its origin and completion in these three dynamics. Faith and obedience bridge the divine and the human, allowing the Church to manifest the will of God on earth as it is in heaven.

The Church is not merely a physical institution; it is fundamentally a spiritual entity. This means its essence and existence are rooted in the spiritual realm, and spiritual principles guide its operations and functions. This dual nature is vital to understand, as the spiritual takes preeminence over the physical. Every legitimate function within the physical church manifests from what has already been established in the heavenly realm. The Church operates as a vessel through which God administers His will by the Holy Spirit, engaging the saints through their faith and obedience in love.

The Manifestation of the visible evidence of God's work is not arbitrary. It is the completion of a divine operation. Before this visible outcome occurs, conditions must be fulfilled on both ends: God initiates the work in heaven by His promises, and believers participate through faith and obedience on earth. This collaborative process reveals the deeply interwoven relationship between Christ and his Church.

God, who is a spirit, created man in His likeness and entrusted him with the authority to operate within his physical nature by God's holiness and divine will. Man, endowed with dominion as seen in Adam, was subject to the boundaries set by God. However, man sought to surpass these boundaries, resulting in the loss of his dominion in God's will. This transgression necessitated a spiritual intervention to restore man. In essence, through disobedience, man forfeited his authority to subdue the earth, command its creatures, and exercise dominion over creation. Consequently, God intervened to reinstate operational authority in the natural world despite being a spirit.

It is essential to understand that God's sovereign will does not depend on man's obedience but on His decree. In His omniscience, God foresaw man's weakness within His divine plan—He may allow the rise of a Saul while predestining a David.

Man, being spiritually dead, cannot engage with a holy God. To bridge this gap, God acted through Christ, uniting us in the last Adam. Through Christ, Lordship was established, holding full authority over heaven and earth, with the power to operate in both realms. However, the focus is not on man but on Christ, the incarnate Son of God, from whom the Church derives its purpose and function. Therefore, God's will is carried out through the Spirit of Christ, with the Church serving as the vessel of His authority, demonstrated by the faith and obedience of believers. Christ holds authority in heaven and on earth through His life, death, and resurrection, enabling the Church to function as His body and exercise His authority on earth.

The Church's effectiveness relies on believers' alignment with Christ through faith and obedience. Christ is the central figure who validates and empowers every function of the Church. However, believers are not passive bystanders in this process. From the foundation of the world, God chose His people to participate in this unfolding mystery (Ephesians 1:4-10) actively. This participatory role highlights the close relationship God desires with His Church.

Practical Implications for the Modern Church

Understanding these principles carries profound practical implications for the contemporary Church. It is not just about belief but about how we live out our faith and obedience in our daily lives and the life of the Church. The following are areas of practical obedience:

- **Corporate Worship and Unity:** Faith and obedience foster genuine worship and unity. Worship is more than ritual; it is an act of faith, recognizing God's sovereignty and responding in obedience to His commands. Unity in worship reflects the spiritual reality of the Church's oneness in Christ, transcending denominational and cultural divides. When believers gather in faith and humility, the Church mirrors the heavenly assembly, bringing glory to God.
- **Mission and Evangelism:** The Church's mission flows directly from Christ's Great Commission. Faith prompts believers to trust in God's power to save, while obedience compels them to take action. Evangelism is not optional but a natural outworking of faith and obedience. As the Church proclaims the gospel, it aligns with God's desire to bring all things under Christ (Ephesians 1:10).
- **Stewardship and Service:** Faith and obedience are demonstrated through the responsible management of resources and the service to others. The early Church demonstrated this in Acts 2:42-47, where believers shared all their possessions to ensure that no one was in need. This radical generosity was motivated not by obligation but by faith in God's provision and obedience to Christ's teachings.

Modern churches that reflect this spirit serve as a testament to God's kingdom, offering a powerful witness to the world.

- **Spiritual Gifts and Ministry:** Ephesians 4 highlights the diversity of gifts within the body of Christ. Faith allows believers to recognize and embrace their spiritual gifts, while obedience ensures these gifts are used properly to edify the Church. The operation of spiritual gifts reflects divine administration, where each member functions according to God's design, contributing to the growth and maturity of the Church.
- **Discipleship and Growth:** The call to make disciples is a direct application of faith and obedience. Faith trusts in the transformative power of God's Word, while obedience teaches, mentors, and guides us and others in our walk with Christ. A Church grounded in discipleship mirrors Christ's ministry, producing fruit that endures.
- **Perseverance in Trials:** Faith and obedience sustain the Church during persecution and hardship. Historically, the Church has thrived not in comfort but in adversity, where believers' unwavering faith and steadfast obedience became a testimony to God's grace. This principle remains crucial today as the Church navigates societal pressures and spiritual opposition.

The Overarching Purpose is unity in Christ. The recurring theme in Ephesians is clear: In Christ, through Christ, by Christ. God's ultimate purpose is to bring unity to all things in heaven and on earth under Christ (Ephesians 1:10). This unity is both the goal and the fruit of faith and obedience. As the body of Christ, the Church plays a pivotal role in bringing this divine plan to fruition. As believers walk in faith and obedience, they participate in God's redemptive work, demonstrating His glory to the world.

Faith and obedience are not abstract concepts but lived realities that shape the Church's mission, worship, service, and unity. As the

Church anchors itself in Christ, it becomes a visible expression of God's kingdom, fulfilling His will on earth as it is in heaven.

The Mystery of Christ and the Church

Unity, growth, and love are revealed here: "Christ in you, the hope of glory."

Colossians 1:26-27 discusses the mystery that was hidden for ages but is now made known to God's people. This mystery, Christ in you, the hope of glory, shows the transformative truth for Gentiles who were once under the power of sin and death, led astray by the god of this world—Satan. "... *Having no hope and without God in this world. But now in Christ Jesus, you who were far off have been brought near by the blood of Christ.*" Ephesians 2:12,13

As Gentiles, we once held authority as humans on earth, possessing inalienable rights, yet we were under the influence of the spirit of this world, led by sin and bound to the spirit of death. However, we have been redeemed at a great price and brought into the Kingdom of God, where we have received the Spirit of grace and the privilege to perceive His kingdom.

In 1 Corinthians 12:2, Paul reminds us, "Ye know that ye were Gentiles, carried away unto these dumb idols, even as ye were led." Though idols are lifeless and powerless to lead, another spirit—the enemy of God—manipulates our physical and legal privileges, drawing glory to Satan, the "god of this world." This adversary influences nations and systems, exercising dominion over those who remain under his sway.

However, as believers, we are no longer of this world; its influence no longer leads us. We are brought under His rule and liberated from death's power by the Spirit of Christ. Paul continues in verse 3, "*Wherefore I give you to understand, that no man speaking by the Spirit of God calleth Jesus accursed.*" Why? Because our spiritual eyes have been opened by faith, we no longer perceive Jesus through the flesh or from a worldly perspective. Christ is no longer a stumbling block to us; He is revealed as Lord and no longer seen as one accursed.

I have often encountered questions rooted in speculation and misunderstanding, many of which are inspired by apocryphal writings, that cast doubt on Christ's earthly life. For example, some ask, "How do we know that Jesus never had relations with a woman while on earth?" Even among professing Christians, the answer sometimes echoes, "We can never know," while others falsely claim He did. In both instances, they have called Jesus accursed.

My point is that understanding who Jesus truly is—both in His humanity and His present glory as Lord—is essential to grounding our faith. To know Him rightly is to begin grasping the mystery of His identity. Our sinful nature found no occasion in Him, and the universal fate of men did not dictate His death but was a deliberate act of obedience to the Father. Unlike all others, whose death is inevitable under sin's dominion, Jesus chose to submit to death by divine purpose.

Philippians 2:7-8 declares, *"He took upon him the form of a servant... and being found in fashion as a man, he humbled himself and became obedient unto death."* This obedience was not to death itself but unto God, even to the point of death. The curse of sin forces Man to be obedient to death, but Christ's obedience was to the Father, making His death an act of willing surrender. This distinction is profound.

We, too, must now walk in a new obedience, no longer compelled by the fear of death but led by the Holy Spirit. Paul concludes, *"No man can say that Jesus is Lord but by the Holy Ghost."* Through the Spirit's revelation, we confess Christ's Lordship, not as a mere doctrine, but as the foundation of our transformed lives, in union, fellowship, and love.

Ephesians 4:7-8, 12 states: *"But unto every one of us is given grace according to the measure of the gift of Christ. Wherefore he said, when he ascended up on high, he led captivity captive, and gave gifts to men... for the perfecting of the saints, for the work of the ministry, for the edifying of the body of Christ."*

We, who were once captives and led astray, have been delivered and are now equipped to follow the Spirit of God as members of His body— the full manifestation of His perfect love. This divine love cannot be fully expressed by one person alone but finds its fulfillment in unity as many become one. When God created Man in His image and likeness, He did not leave them as solitary beings but fashioned them as both male and female, distinct yet united.

This mystery of unity and distinction was prefigured from the very beginning. Genesis 1:27 reveals this profound truth: *"So God created man in his own image, in the image of God created he him; male and female created he them."*

Later, in Genesis 2:18, it is written: *"And the Lord God said, it is not good that the man should be alone; I will make him a helpmeet for him."*

The Hebrew phrase suggests a companion "corresponding to him," reflecting the unity in God's design. Adam affirms this in Genesis 2:23: *"This is now bone of my bones and flesh of my flesh: she shall be called Woman because she was taken out of Man."*

This union foreshadows the mystery Paul unveils in Ephesians 3:9: *"To bring to light for everyone what is the plan of the mystery hidden for ages in God who created all things."*

Ephesians 5 further expands on this mystery, describing the believer's walk toward spiritual maturity, culminating in true fellowship. Paul writes in Ephesians 5:21: *"Submitting yourselves one to another in the fear of God."*

Verses 22-33 illustrate the covenant of marriage as a reflection of Christ's relationship with the Church. Paul draws a direct parallel, saying:
"For we are members of his body, of his flesh, and of his bones. For this cause shall a man leave his father and mother and be joined unto his wife, and they two shall be one flesh. This is a great mystery, but I speak concerning Christ and the Church."

This echoes Genesis 2:23, reinforcing that the marital union reflects the more excellent mystery of Christ and His Church. Colossians 1:26 also references this mystery, which has been hidden for ages but is now revealed. The fellowship of believers mirrors the intimacy of marriage, albeit without sensuality, reflecting a spiritual oneness.

At the heart of this mystery is the concept of divine union. As Jesus declares in Matthew 22:29-30: *"Ye do err, not knowing the scriptures, nor the power of God. For in the resurrection they neither marry, nor are given in marriage, but are as the angels of God in heaven."*

In the resurrection, the need for growth and demonstration of love through union will cease, for the imperfections of the flesh will be no more. Yet in the present age, through the covenant of marriage or the new covenant of life in Christ, our differences and unique gifts cultivate interdependence, allowing love to flourish even in imperfection.

The Church reflects this by divine design—a fellowship of diverse members, each needing the other to reveal the whole nature of the body of Christ. Through this sacred interdependence, the Church embodies true love and unity.

Growing in Love Through Suffering, Submission, and Fellowship

Love is perfect and relational, yet imperfect beings are called to grow into this ideal love. Our diverse gifts and interdependence fuel this growth. When God declared, "It is not good for man to be alone" in Genesis 2, He was not merely addressing isolation but the inability of one person alone to enjoy the union of love. Humanity, "all in one," could not walk in the concert of love or true fellowship.

As fallen beings, our challenge is no longer to walk in love but to mature and grow in love through obedience and suffering. Suffering becomes the threshold where choice determines whether we remain bound to our old nature or ascend to more significant growth in love. Even Christ exemplified this: *"Though he was a Son, yet learned he obedience by the things which he suffered."* – Hebrews 5:8

How Is This Growth in Love Accomplished?

Paul answers this in Ephesians 4:7-13 (KJV): *"But unto every one of us is given grace according to the measure of the gift of Christ. Wherefore he saith, when he ascended up on high, he led* captivity captive, and gave gifts unto men... Till we all come in the unity of the faith, and of the knowledge of the Son of God, unto a perfect man, unto the measure of the stature of the fullness of Christ."

The word "till" in Ephesians 4:13 reveals a process of sanctification and growth, transitioning from a disobedient spirit to love. This growth occurs through submission and obedience. However, obedience to God can often feel unclear when directed directly during this process of "till." During this process, we submit to the fellowship and doctrine of the Church, guided by those entrusted to lead (the presbytery), because to us, during this process of "till," obedience to God is a murky thing.

Paul explains this further in 1 Corinthians 12:1-3 (ESV): "Now concerning spiritual gifts, brothers, I do not want you to be uninformed. You know that when you were pagans you were led astray to mute idols, however you were led. Therefore, I want you to understand that no one speaking in the Spirit of God ever says 'Jesus is accursed,' and no one can say 'Jesus is Lord' except in the Holy Spirit."

James also highlights the internal conflict within believers: "From whence come wars and fightings among you? Come they not hence, even of your lusts that war in your members?" – James 4:1 (KJV)

The Spirit of God within us desires our full devotion, but our old nature resists. James 4:5 (ESV) adds, "He yearns jealously over the spirit that he has made to dwell in us."

The Process of Growth (Till We All Come...)

Though God has given us His Spirit and spiritual gifts, our old nature prevents us from fully yielding to the Holy Spirit. As Paul states in 1 Corinthians 12:7 (NLT): "A spiritual gift is given to each of us as a means of helping the entire church."

Until our faith matures and becomes steadfast, we remain vulnerable to the desires and conflicts within us. This is why Paul emphasizes the necessity of spiritual gifts for the edification of the body:

"And he gave some, apostles; and some, prophets; and some,

evangelists; and some, pastors and teachers; for the perfecting of the saints, for the work of the ministry, for the edifying of the body of Christ: Till..." – Ephesians 4:11-13

During this "till," we yield to those gifts in submission to the body of Christ:

"And I will give you pastors according to mine heart, which shall feed you with knowledge and understanding." – Jeremiah 3:15

This process of "till" leads to, *"The unity of the faith, and of the knowledge of the Son of God, unto a perfect man, unto the measure of the stature of the fullness of Christ."* – Ephesians 4:13

As we grow individually, the corporate body matures, increasing the Church's capacity to love and reflect Christ's fullness.

Paul warns against remaining spiritual infants: *"That we henceforth be no more children, tossed to and fro, and carried about with every wind of doctrine, by the sleight of men, and cunning craftiness, whereby they lie in wait to deceive."* – Ephesians 4:14

Instead, through love and truth, we grow into Christ, the head of the Church:

"But speaking the truth in love, may grow up into him in all things, which is the head, even Christ." – Ephesians 4:15

As members of the body, we must understand that even powerful spiritual gifts must function within the order and submission of the Church. This submission is not arbitrary but aligned with the growth and benefit of the body in love.

Thus, we submit to one another as members of Christ's body, fostering unity and maturity so the Church may become a whole habitation of God's love.

However, the contemporary Church often functions more as a natural entity, divided by denominational camps rather than unified by the Spirit. True unity is rooted in submission to the Spirit of Christ, fostering collective growth.

To reconcile the Church with its primary objective, the Church's function must transcend earthly structures and legacy-driven models. Our modern claims of apostolic succession and denominational pride can obscure the universal unity intended for the Body. At its core, the Church is one, holy, and apostolic, sustained not by human effort but by divine grace.

The universal nature of the Church is evident when believers walk in the Spirit, aligning with Christ's mind and Word. This results in organic growth and obedience, reflecting the self-healing nature of the Body.

The preceding view of "The Functioning of the Church" may seem abstract and impractical to our norms. However, the challenge lies in reconciling the primary objective and function of the Body with the contemporary Church. The structure and functioning of the Church have increasingly evolved to serve our corporal legacy and spiritual needs under the guise of apostolic succession or generational legacy. We have replaced the transcendence of the Church, which defines spirituality, with natural administrators, rituals, and pseudo-spirituality. In many cases, the physical representation of the Church today has become a natural entity, and, practically speaking, it is comprised of multiple entities. This fractures the unity of the faith, reducing it to camps of belief.

At the inception of the Church, Catholicity and Orthodoxy were distinctions of universal acknowledgment and submission to true apostolicity, not denominational primacy. This unity was not the result of human effort but rather a transcendent gift of grace. If such unity rests on human ideals, we must examine whether we are indeed in the Faith. If we trust in His Word and His grace, but unity is still lacking, we should question whether we are faithful to Scripture and the Body. Proper submission to the Spirit of Christ inherently fosters unity and edification.

Like the human body, the Church grows and heals when adequately nourished. Scripture, centered on Christ, serves as the corrective measure when the Church diverges. *"Behold, I have come—In the volume of the book it is written of Me—To do Your will, O God."* As the Church, we must correct and align ourselves through unity.

The Great Commission begins with *"All power is given unto me in heaven and in earth."* This authority ensures the doctrinal purpose of Scripture to instruct and correct (2 Timothy 3:16, Romans 15:4) alongside Christ's command to teach His ways. His perpetual presence, *"I am with you always, even unto the end of the world,"* empowers the Church.

This power dwells within each believer. As members of the Body, each one is accountable to God by grace and to the Church by their gifts. The Church functions through collective maturity, united by one Spirit, one Faith, and one Salvation, leading to obedience and growth.

Chapter 9

Your Function in the Church

Simon Peter, a bondservant and apostle of Jesus Christ,
*To those who have received a **faith** of the same kind as ours, by the righteousness of our God and Savior, Jesus Christ:* ^{2}*Grace and peace be multiplied to you in the **knowledge** of God and of Jesus our Lord;* ^{3}*seeing that His divine power has granted to us everything pertaining to life and godliness, through the **true knowledge** of Him who called us by His own glory and excellence.* ^{4}*For by these He has granted to us His precious and magnificent promises, so that by them you may become partakers of the divine nature, having escaped the corruption that is in the world by lust.* ^{5}*Now for this very reason also, applying all diligence, in your faith supply **moral excellence**, and in your moral excellence, knowledge,*
   - 2 Peter 1:1-5, NASB

9A

To examine the third aspect of the Church, we may ask: how do I participate in this functioning, and by what means?

2 Peter begins with "Simon Peter," a servant and apostle of Jesus Christ. He identifies himself with humility and authority. Addressing "those who have received a faith (pistis) of the same kind (or as precious) as ours," he emphasizes the equal value of the faith that unites us in the body of Christ. Recognizing the precious nature of this gift, we receive it regardless of our station, not by our own merit, but "by the righteousness of our God and Savior Jesus Christ."

In verse two, he introduced a key term: epignosis (knowledge) – a deep revealed knowledge of God, which refers to God's recognition or divine revelation. This is not simply intellectual agreement; it is spiritual recognition. Furthermore, faith is not just an inner disposition but the response to divine revelation. As Peter declared, grace and peace are multiplied through this knowledge. Now the "faith" (pistis) we receive is both the acknowledgment of this revelation and the strength to endure by grace. This knowledge is inseparable from the faith we have received, and the faith is inseparable from knowing Him.

In modern usage, the word 'faith' does not fully describe the origin of our belief but rather our engagement with it. Left to its own devices, it can lead to disconnected religious practice and a lack of conviction or proper understanding. As a safeguard, verses 1-4 explain the source and means by which we partake in this faith, leading us to verse 3.

Verse 3 clearly states, *"His divine power has granted us everything necessary for life and godliness,"* that is, *"through the true knowledge of Him"*—again, epignosis— an imprinted, revelatory knowledge of *"Him who called us by His own glory and excellence (goodness)."* Our calling is based on God's intrinsic goodness and power, not human merit.

Moving on to verse 4.

*For **by these** (*His excellence and divine power*) He has granted to us* [a] *His precious and magnificent promises.* Why? *"so that by them you* may become _partakers of the divine nature_, having _escaped the corruption_ that is in the world through lust."

God describes His gifts as _"His precious and magnificent promises,"_ emphasizing their importance. As the underlined parts show, He provided us with everything related to life and godliness: first, for fellowship with Him through a return to worship; second, for freedom from our sinful nature, so that we may share in His holiness.

So, verses 1-4 describe our intimate encounter with God through revelation and grace by faith. We respond with a renewed moral choice, or in a sense, a new willpower, to believe and live transformed lives.

In verse 5, there is a shift from the provision to the application. _"Now for this very reason also, applying all diligence..."_ building on what we received: _"in your faith supply moral excellence."_ This highlights the functioning of faith. The Key Word Study Bible defines this faith as accepting what God in Christ offers, leading to the transformation of man's character and lifestyle.

We must provide moral excellence, but this is the problem. When I look inward and realize I am not reflecting Christ, I find that the account of faith is present, but the supply of moral excellence or virtue is lacking. Therefore, the issue is not necessarily in doctrine or unity among the brethren (though these may be absent); it is not an inherently corporate problem, and all the religious piety and doctrine cannot provide an essential fix, but must come from our internal reform.

We must continually reflect on our condition, acknowledge our sins, and pursue repentance and the grace necessary to develop our moral excellence. This virtue must originate from our faith, reflecting our experiences and life in God's presence. It is not just about knowing and understanding God but about experiencing and receiving His grace in a way that goes beyond our mental faculties and defines the wisdom in our walk. In other words, sanctification.

Therefore, considering this, the Body's function must originate from its members, those who are called regeneratively. Born of God's Spirit and transformed through sanctification of the soul and renewal of the mind. This transformation leads to the revival of the Word, where God's Spirit can establish a foundation in those called. Only then do doctrine (theology), vision, and religion emerge as personal or local mandates or representatives. There, grace shows up in the ability to fulfill the purpose for which you are called, accompanied by multiplied Grace and Peace that drive that purpose. However, all this must come from the kind of encounter described above: a revelatory impartation of faith and knowledge of God, which enables us to share a common vision as we walk together by the Word and the Spirit.

Through this, the Church is called to a genuine spiritual duty. It is more a natural result of a relational experience or transformation than just an intellectual or rational ascent—a reality hidden from the wise and clever and revealed to the humble.

This knowledge of God fosters an indelible awe that erodes and replaces the trust and confidence we once had in ourselves and humanity, making us aware of the depths of His grace. We realize we have been called to something far beyond our natural ambitions and talents, yet we pursue it. Furthermore, although we recognize it is not our innate desires driving us, it has become our ever-growing zeal, and by our own choice, we follow the will of God. Regarding the collective remedy, it will begin to self-adjust as its members adopt the identity of this new passion and fulfill their proper roles.

Peter continues, "...and in your moral excellence, knowledge." Building on that goodness, knowledge—not epignosis, but gnosis— references to intellectual, doctrinal, and practical understanding. However, even this knowledge must be accompanied by faith and moral transformation. Why? Because knowledge without virtue leads to arrogance or pride, but knowledge gained through virtue is rooted in humility, by the grace of God. It teaches us what is required and what must change within us. This transformation by grace enables us to incorporate self-control into this knowledge and avoid stumbling.

This is where it comes into play to "work out your own salvation with fear and trembling." Faith is a gift of grace, but virtue is developed through internal transformation of that faith, as our minds are renewed daily, receiving what is given to us in verse 3 ("everything necessary for life and godliness"). Before we received the Holy Spirit, we could not choose anything that yielded righteous fruits. However, now the two desires of the old and new natures continue battling in your mind. Now you have faith; you know His Son and trust His Word. Now, exercise that faith and begin to choose. Every choice we make to trust God carries an inherent power to overcome, and as we grow in character, our control over the carnal nature increases; this is virtue.

We are also instructed to add knowledge to our virtue, not only knowing what is required of us but also allowing the Word to reveal the areas in the flesh we need to overcome. Combine that knowledge with virtue, and what do we get? Control over the flesh, self-control, and temperance. With continuous use of your self-control, you can walk in patience and long-suffering, keeping the passions of the flesh under subjection until that victory is achieved. When the passions of the flesh are controlled, the desires of the Spirit will prevail; thus, the Spirit now holds the rod of choice, and you can walk with the renewed mind of the Spirit. It is the Spirit that can add godliness to your patience. You can now think as God thinks, not to be like Him or possess His thoughts, but to do so with a godly approach, not haste in decisions and judgments, but by bearing with the burdens of men. By doing this, we can consistently show kindness to one another, thereby adding to our godliness, brotherly kindness. To maintain brotherly kindness, you will need to endure the challenges of mankind for as long as it takes, accept others as more than yourself, and be content. Do not focus solely on your own interests, but remain humble, walking with your fellow man in light of their circumstances before God, and add to your brotherly kindness love.

1 Corinthians 13:6 says, "Love rejoices, *not in iniquity but in truth*."

When truth entered, many believers rejoiced in the salvation of grace; grace abounds, and we stopped short of love because we thought we were walking in love. However, the love we boast about is brotherly kindness. While we genuinely persist, we frustrate the grace of God; we boast in love, but in truth, we rejoice in iniquity. Grace entered, but the truth is often resisted, as shown by our fruits. We must move beyond kindness into the fullness of love, lest we frustrate the grace of God and become blind, short-sighted, and forget the very deliverance we have received, according to 2 Peter 1:9.

You may notice that the Bible often uses the term 'perfect' instead of 'mature' to describe certain stages in a person's walk before God. I believe this translation reflects God's intent. A person is not perfect before God, but they persevere and endure. 1 Corinthians 13:7-8, speaking of love, says: "Beareth all things, believeth all things, hopeth all things, endureth all things. Love never fails." This represents the perfection of persistence.

In 2 Peter, there are two instances of the phrase "to be diligent," first in adding virtue or moral excellence to our faith in verse 5, which remains in effect and continues through verse 7 until you add love. Then verse 8 states, "For if these qualities are yours and are increasing, they render you neither useless nor unfruitful in the true knowledge of our Lord Jesus Christ."

We are returning to verses two and three, epignosis, a true revelation of Christ. In another place, I mentioned revelation not as knowledge to be acquired and retained through our faculties but as an imprint on our soul and a state of change in our spirit. However, when we quench the Spirit, we also lose the outworking of this imprint. This brings us to verse 9: *"For the one who lacks these qualities is blind or short-sighted, having forgotten his purification from his former sins."*

Remember when Jesus said, "No man after putting his hand to the plow and looking back is fit for the kingdom of God," in Luke 9:62? In verse 10, this diligence is called for again: *"Therefore, brothers and sisters, be all the more diligent to make certain about His calling and choice of you; for as long as you practice these things, you will never stumble."*

As we have received this precious faith in verse one, we continue to pursue it. It is not a token to hold onto, but a faith to walk out. So, if, by your belief, you think you have received the faith and are just waiting for the redemption of the body, it may be that you have received a pseudo-righteousness. *"All the more, be diligent to make certain of His calling and your choice of Him."* I am confident that this language does not imply that if you can persist, then He will let you in. That would be works righteousness, and grace would not be grace. The certainty of the calling is for our benefit and understanding. Verse 10 starts with *"therefore,"* referring to verses 5-7: *"if these qualities are yours and are increasing"* from verse 8, *"they do not make you useless and unproductive in the true knowledge of our Lord Jesus Christ,"* which concludes with verse 11, *"for in this way the entrance into the eternal kingdom of our Lord and Savior Jesus Christ will be abundantly supplied to you,"*

This passage can be seen as the final entry granted to the believer into the kingdom of heaven, and while that is true, it also signifies an entry while still in mortal flesh. The thief on the cross next to Christ was barely saved, and Christ told him, "Today you will be with me in paradise." Paradise is a union of completion; there is no ongoing ministry or partial access. Notice the text says, "an entrance shall be ministered (a serviced or temporary supply of access) unto you abundantly... (abounding is only required in the mortal vessel, not in that eternal vessel). That entrance began with true knowledge, the revelation of the Lord Jesus Christ. In the case of the thief, he was at death's door, and his revelation and entry were completed in that hour when Jesus said, "Today you will be with me in paradise." - There was no abundance of grace from virtue to love for the thief. However, our entry is ministered by abundant grace through retaining that revelatory knowledge and its imprint on our souls. His Spirit continues to quicken our faith until we depart this mortal vessel.

The last part of verse 4 says, "having escaped the corruption that is in the world through lust." Similarly, Proverbs 22:3 states, "A prudent man foresees the evil, and hides himself; but the simple pass on, and are punished." The words in these texts, "escaped" and "hide," imply that not only were we initially trapped, but a trap continues to be set for us; either way, we must choose a path.

Our natural path is inherently corrupt, hence the term escaped. Before we inherited this faith, corruption and punishment were our only options. As fools, we continued in our own way and faced the consequences. - *"The fool says in his heart, 'There is no God.' They are corrupt, they do abominable deeds; there is none who does good."* (Psalm 14:1 ESV).

Then, how do we find the right path? Through the virtue and excellence that come from knowing Him. As we grow in understanding, we learn to trust Him. With self-control, we act on this trust and avoid the corruption in the world caused by lust. - The prudent man sees the evil and hides from it. *"Fear of the Lord is the beginning of wisdom, and knowledge of the Holy One is understanding.* (Proverbs 9:10 NIV)

The final part of verse 4 indicates that we can share in His divine nature by escaping the corruption in the world that is caused by lust. Paul emphasizes this in Romans 7:7, "I had not known sin, but by the law; for I had not known lust, except the law said, thou shalt not covet." We differentiate between these paths through the law. "Thou shalt not covet" is the other side of the coin, with the words of Jesus in Matthew 22:37-40.

Thou shalt love the Lord thy God with all thy heart, and with all thy soul, and with all thy mind...Thou shalt love thy neighbor as thyself. On these two commandments hang all the law and the prophets.

The law teaches us that corruption in the world stems from lust or envy, but escape from this lust is achieved through love. Thus, the law helps us discern our paths, whether in the lust of the flesh or the delight of the Law. Through the Law, we gain a true reflection of ourselves.

As Paul writes in Romans 7:18; *For I know that in me (that is, in my flesh) dwells no good thing.*

Before encountering the law, we believed we were fine. Many still do—people who claim to believe in God and look forward to pleading their case before Him based on their supposed goodness. I am only now realizing how genuine and perilous this mindset is. They are convinced they are okay but do not take Christ at His Word; instead, they anticipate pleading their case before Him. However, through the conviction of the law, we see our guilt, and the deception of sin is exposed. *"I was alive without the law once, but when the commandment came, sin revived, and I died."* Romans 7:9.

Paul, fully aware of his dilemma, cries out, *"O wretched man that I am! Who shall deliver me from the body of this death?"* (Romans 7:24) His response is thanksgiving for deliverance: *"I thank God through Jesus Christ our Lord."* (Vs 25) So, with the mind, he serves the law of God, but with the flesh, the law of sin.

Now, we rejoice in the revelation of the law and the escape from death it brings, but the more we try to evade it, the more we find ourselves trapped by it. The law itself condemns us to death by exposing our deeds, acting as a form of slavery. However, you say we are not under the law but under grace, so let us examine this within the context of grace. A key issue is the misuse of this grace. Under this claim, religion is often exploited by the enemy as another form of the law, reviving sin through performance rituals. Many believers remain enslaved to sin under the cover of grace, repeating the mistake Paul warns against: *"Shall we continue in sin, that grace may abound? God forbid."* Romans 6:1,15.

Generally, this is not because they want to sin but because they believe they have no choice. However, Romans 6:6 contradicts this defeatism. Still, some believe the lie, "There is no escape from the curse until this body is physically redeemed."

Today's congregational culture often emphasizes church attendance, activities, tithing, and similar outward acts. While not inherently wrong, these can become sources of bondage when done out of obligation or to earn God's favor. That is a return to the law. Faithful obedience is not transactional but transformational, rooted in love rather than obligation.

Paul said that with the sinful nature or flesh, he serves the law of sin, but he did not mean to obey sin in its lusts; otherwise, he would be in direct contradiction with himself. This was made clear in the previous chapter (Romans 6). We serve sin in the flesh as a penalty, sharing in Christ's suffering—by the burden of your cross, by which you forfeit the natural gratifications of the sinful nature for the will of God, in thanksgiving through Jesus Christ.

It is possible to outwardly 'do the law' without the inner revelation that sin no longer has power over you. We can still wrestle with a guilty conscience, trying to please God through works rather than faith. However, everything shifts when we truly understand that the law is spiritual and the battle is in the mind.

Paul writes, "*For in my inner being, I delight in God's law; but I see another law at work in me, waging war against the law of my mind...*" (Romans 7:22-23).

Losing that inner battle means remaining a slave to sin. Still, again, this victory does not come through effort or performance, although these can result from it. This victory is deliverance through Christ. Thanks be to God, who delivers me through Jesus Christ our Lord! (v 25)

This is the victory: "So then, I myself in my mind am a slave to God's law." Not only through faith and revelation, but also through deliberate will. This represents the knowledge that complements moral excellence – liberation in the mind from the sinful nature, even though the flesh remains subject to decay.

"*...but in my sinful nature a slave to the law of sin.*"

This liberty is evident through our delight in the law of God (Romans 7:22), further confirmed in Romans 8, which states that Christ condemned (past tense) sin in the flesh. In contrast, the unbeliever remains captive; the conscience testifies to their guilt. Their only option now is to acknowledge their guilt before God, surrendering to the fact that they are worthy of death. Only then can you kneel in your heart to the mercies of God, through the revelation that by Grace, you are saved and redeemed from under the law.

When we follow the law under grace, it is not for earning salvation but glorifying God. The law now functions as a measuring stick for grace because "without the law there is no transgression." When the law reveals sin, grace becomes even greater, since grace only meets us where sin is acknowledged. Under Moses, the law made redemption visible, but it was never sufficient for eternal life, because the wages of sin is death. The law governs a system that leads to death unless grace intervenes.

Paul asks, "Was then that which is good made death unto me?" No – it was sin, that through the commandment might appear exceedingly sinful (Romans 7:13). That is, sin reveals its full ugliness under the light of the law, so that grace might be fully known. The law of Moses did not give us a new choice but exposed the one already made in Adam. Hence, the law says, "Thou shalt not..." accompanied by sacrifices. But how can we "not" when we are already guilty? By dying. By substitutionary death, sin is undone.

Grace fulfills the law in our flesh through the blood of Jesus. It restores life both spiritually and legally by the resurrected Christ and seals us with the Spirit. Romans 8:15 states, *"For ye have not the spirit of bondage again to fear; but ye have received the Spirit of adoption, whereby we cry, 'Abba Father.'"*

Yet James reminds us: *"The Spirit that dwells in us lusts to envy"* (James 4:5). The Holy Spirit desires to possess us as completely as sin once did, with the throne of covetousness. Victory is only achieved when the reigning power is dethroned.

"No one can say Jesus is Lord but by the Holy Spirit."

So, how do we partake of those divine promises?

2 Peter 1:3 states that His divine power has given us everything we need for life and godliness through the knowledge of Him who called us to His own glory and virtue. That glory has existed from the beginning, but our virtue—our moral excellence needs to reflect it. This is why verse 10 encourages us to "Give all diligence to make our calling and election sure: for if ye do these things, ye shall never fall."

We observed that once sin was imputed through the law, it condemned every part of our lives. Death seemed to prevail in both life and death. But Peter offers a different perspective: a faith that guarantees we are never barren or unproductive. This confidence does not come from performance but from growth through grace.

2 Peter 1:5-8 describes this growth:
- Add to your faith, virtue [grace begins to abound]
- To virtue, knowledge [understanding what God has prepared for us]
- To knowledge, temperance [mastery over the flesh]
- To temperance, patience [continuing in well doing]
- To patience, godliness [knowing (living in) the acceptable way of the Lord]
- To godliness, brotherly kindness [relational and individual consideration]
- To brotherly kindness, charity [genuine love for others]

These qualities are not based on preferences or convenience but are essential and inherent to faith. Love is defined by action and genuine, relational expressions, not identity. You cannot legislate love; that will only create the appearance of it. True love requires moral judgment and a willing choice.

Despite 2 Peter's hopeful tone, the struggle with the law persists because lust and envy remain within us. The fight of the will continues: the fleshly nature once dominated under the law, and sin deceived us into death. However, now, the believer grows—not in fear but in complete confidence—having escaped the corruption in the world caused by lust.

Chapter 10

Knowing and executing your duty

*"For through the grace given to me I say to everyone among you not to think more highly of himself than he ought to **think**; but to think so as to have sound judgment, as God has allotted to each a measure of faith. For just as we have many members in one body and all the members do not have the same **function**, so we, who are many, are one body in Christ, and **individually** members one of another. Since we have gifts that differ according to the grace given to us, each of us is to exercise them accordingly: if prophecy, according to the **proportion** of his faith."*
— Romans 12:3–6

What Is Required of Us?

What is required of us and how we execute those duties is answered in two parts. The answer to the first part is **obedience to our faith**; I am not speaking about obedience to mere law and doctrine, which at one time was necessary, but rather personal obedience. What do I mean by personal obedience?

The obedience of your fear. Here, the fear that fuels this obedience is reverence for God. It is an obedience that is measured by what or how much you are willing to suffer or lose to maintain God's presence.

Peace with, and the presence of God, becomes more valuable and desirable than personal satisfaction and worldly pursuits. This stems not from mere obligation, but from a place of eventual recognition on your part, sanctified by grace. It involves weaving a faith that remains strong with the proper perspective of our humble state before God. This obedience is born from personal experience and growth in your relationship with God. During this growth process, God may require you to endure suffering under the law to glorify Christ through you.

The phrase "the obedience of your fear" may sound contrary to faith, but this is what most Christians refer to as faith. It is not the faith of manifestation or "substance," but the faith of growth. This process teaches you to recognize the measure of faith given to you. Remember, the gifts we receive are primarily for the body, and due to our selfish nature, we often do not recognize what lies outside our self-interest and inherently do not want to. This is why you pray and cry for the things you need, and He hears you; however, you do not receive because need must be viewed in the context of the Body. So, this is not a time for receiving, but for growing up.

According to our text, verse 3 gives us the framework for measuring our faith:

"Not to think more highly of yourself than you ought to think, but to think so as to have sound judgment, as God has allotted to each a measure of faith."

The Greek word for "ought to think" (phroneō) means to exercise the mind, form an opinion, and intentionally direct one's mindset, even in matters of concern or obedience. This indicates that we must deliberately examine our motives, submit our will, and view ourselves with sober reflection. From this humility, we perceive the accurate measure of our faith and the discernment needed to exercise sound judgment.

One Body, Many Members – Yet United in Christ

Verse 4 says.

"For just as we have many members in one body and all the members do not have the same function..."

This function question was also partly the focus of the previous chapter and remains central to our understanding. However, this verse sets this chapter apart from the previous one, because while each of us is built up individually, we function together as one.

The verse continues:

"So we, who are many, are one body in Christ, and individually members one of another."

This unity of function and diversity of role leads us to the example and ministry of Christ Himself.

Hebrews 5:5-10 says:

5 That is why Christ did not honor himself by assuming he could become High Priest. No, he was chosen by God, who said to him, "You are my Son. Today I have become your Father."

6 And in another passage, God said to him, "You are a priest forever in the order of Melchizedek."

This priestly calling of Christ reflects the spiritual epignosis—revelatory knowledge—we are called to embody as a holy priesthood. Just as Jesus did not appoint Himself but was appointed by God, our calling and purpose must arise from divine revelation, not self-ascribed roles. Likewise, Jesus also had to go through the process of growth in obedience to moral excellence. Except this moral excellence was not for His sake, but for our inheritance on the other side of His resurrection. As he said, *"... For thus it is fitting for us to fulfill all righteousness."*

The Suffering of Obedience

7 While Jesus was here on earth, he offered prayers and pleadings, with a loud cry and tears, to the one who could rescue him from death. And God heard his prayers because of his deep reverence for God.

8 Even though Jesus was God's Son, he learned obedience from the things he suffered.

Here, we see Christ humanly apprehending the necessity of His death through suffering. "Suffering" in this context goes far beyond enduring pain; it encompasses a full range of growth-enabling experiences—what was allowed, required, endured, borne, or deprived. These experiences are not determined by human perceptions of good or bad but are defined by faith, in alignment with God's will and purpose.

9 And, having been made perfect [complete], He became the source of eternal salvation to all who obey Him.

10 And God designated Him to be a High Priest in the order of Melchizedek.

This completed work highlights the priestly aspect of His ministry, the head from which we, as the Body, receive our divine calling. This leads me to the second part of our answer—the grace of our faith.

Functioning According to True Knowledge of Him

Our effectiveness, both as the Body and as individuals, must be rooted in the Word and empowered by the Holy Spirit. However, this must originate from a deep, experiential knowledge of Him—an understanding that encompasses both spirit and truth, as discussed in the previous chapter. This kind of encounter sustains the ministry of Christ through the grace and extent of the gifts He imparts to us.

*"Since we have gifts that differ according to the grace given to us, each of us is to exercise them accordingly: if prophecy, according to the **proportion** of his faith." - (Romans 12:6)*

The word "proportion" comes from the Greek analogía—a compound of ana (distribution) and logos (account). This term appears only here in the New Testament. It suggests that we should exercise our spiritual gifts in proportion to our faith (pistis) to the extent that we can understand and live out the truth revealed to us, grounded in the "true knowledge (epignosis) of Him." This proportion serves as a conduit through which grace flows. Whether the gift is exercised by divine revelation, informed conscience, or a sense of necessary justice, each is distributed by the Word and made effective through Christ.

Christ is the vine; we are the branches. All function, all power, all growth come from Him.

A Sidebar of Personal Experience

- In my early years as a Christian, much of my walk felt like a mountaintop experience. But as I grow in Christ, I am increasingly called to live out my faith through practical words and deeds. Greater responsibility now rests on me to walk in step with the evidence of His grace and gifts in my life. I must learn to make better choices from a heart aligned with His will, knowing that my spirit is subject to my moral agency (1 Corinthians 14:32).

We know *"we have different gifts according to the grace given to us,"* according to Romans 12:6. However, 1 Corinthians 14:32 tells us that the spirit of the prophet is subject to the prophet. So, what indicates to us that we are positioned in His will? Our main text speaks of our reasonable service as a living sacrifice, holy and pleasing to God. Moreover, in Philippians 4:5, Paul says, *"Let your reasonableness be **known to everyone**,"* by rejoicing always in the Lord, with a double emphasis on rejoice.

I think it is safe to tie our reasonable service to our reasonableness, and therefore our joy in the Lord, to our holy and acceptable living, which is our sacrifice to God. As we continue to tie Romans 12 to Philippians 4, Romans 12:6 says that we have gifts according to the grace given. Verses 7 and 8 tell us we walk in that grace in proportion to faith. Well, Philippians 4 tells us how to measure this proportion. Verse 6 says, *"Do not be anxious about anything, but in **everything**, by prayer and supplication with thanksgiving, let your requests be known to God."*

First, we go to God in humility and thanksgiving, and the indicator of our reasonable service, which is the measure of our faith, is the peace that He gives us, as verse 7 indicates. Not our peace. A *"peace which surpasses all understanding."* This peace goes beyond our reasonable service or reason, to grace. The verse finishes with, *"will guard your heart and mind in Christ Jesus."* It is a peace that encompasses our desires, will, and knowledge; our faith in Christ Jesus to affirm whether we operate "according to the grace given to each of us."

Often, we zealously engage in tasks tied to our gifts out of goodwill, obligation, or in pursuit of clarity about our calling. However, the true nature of our work is revealed by our peace in love. The authenticity of that love—whether it flows from the peace of God or fades into frustration—will eventually reveal our true motives: Are we driven by grace and faith, after a genuine desire of the heart, or by duty and ambition?

I say that love will eventually reveal our true motives, because, after starting with the way we ought to think in verse 3, and determining the proportion of our faith through verse 8, Verse 9 produces proof just as Paul calls for evidence at the beginning of our Philippians text with verse 5.

"Let your reasonableness be known to everyone." This is a faith that is made evident across the board.

Or as Romans 12:9 says, "Love must be sincere." This reminds us that love should come from a place of grace, not from burden or obligation, and make our faith evident. As laid out in the rest of the chapter, telling us to *"Abhor that which is evil; cleave to that which is good... Be not overcome of evil, but overcome evil with good."*(KJV). While you may endure trials, the process will refine your gifts and calling, guided by the grace you have received. This grace will be apparent in the ways God requires you to act, infused with the sincerity of love and the persistence of faith, regardless of the challenges you face.

We are now obeying by faith instead of obeying out of fear. This new obedience is rooted in a faith that manifests God's presence in your life, allowing you to witness His grace at work through the power of His substitution.

God is just, and in His justice, He surrendered Himself to the depths of human weakness. This ensures that, in soul, body, or spirit, He has fulfilled the demands of the law of substitution, which includes suffering in the flesh, death, and the judgment of the soul.

Christ was the spotless Lamb. According to His own words, He speaks only what He hears from the Father and does only what He sees the Father do. What, then, does the scripture mean when it says, "He learned obedience by the things which He suffered and was made perfect"? Why did He need to learn obedience, and why specifically through suffering, in order to be made perfect?

Philippians 2:6-7 states, "Who, being in the form of God... was made in the likeness of men." Jesus, although untouched by sin, was fully aware of the depths of human pain. His heart was never desensitized by guilt or corruption, and His conscience was pure. Therefore, He bore our sin and our reproach—our shame and our alienation. The compassion He felt was not weakness but rather the divine sensitivity of perfect love in human form.

We, by contrast, are born into a condition of servitude to sin, not only by nature but also by desire. In our fallen state, we create false gods from anything that promises control or comfort. Only when we are awakened to the truth do we seek redemption. The reality of our subjection is sealed by death, but in Christ, who was "made in the likeness of men," God, in Christ, submitted Himself to our mortality. He relinquished His will to restore us in the Father's will—"Not My will, but Yours be done"—by opening a path through suffering to perfect obedience.

Seeing that it is our obedience, he needed to endure the full extent of human suffering. Learning obedience not from below but from above, laying down divine will to fulfill human submission. This is not a contradiction but divine condescension. His suffering did not make Him imperfect; it made perfect obedience manifest in the flesh, so that we may obey by faith.

Even in His miracles, Christ allowed grace to flow through faith. The woman with the issue of blood did not merely touch Him—she drew on divine virtue. His statement, "I perceive that power has gone out from Me," reveals grace as measurable, receivable, and dispensable according to faith. *"A man receives nothing unless it is given him from heaven"* (John 3:27).

This principle resonates in how we pursue our calling. We may possess zeal, training, and opportunities, but only by grace do we know and fulfill our true duty. Doctrine and law lead us to conviction, but grace lifts us over the threshold into life.

Grace is the spiritual reality that completes the shadow of the law. Even though Christ died for sin, we still die in the body because grace does not work by eliminating the natural process but rather by redeeming it. We suffer daily, dying to our own will, and we live by the will surrendered by Christ. His grace within us empowers obedience, not through human strength but through divine enablement.

Before salvation, we relied on pragmatic human wisdom. However, after conversion, we often feel less skilled in the ways of the world. This is not regression—it is transformation. Human wisdom cannot understand grace, and when we try to operate on that wisdom through faith, we hinder the Spirit of God. James writes, "Such wisdom does not come from above but is earthly, unspiritual, demonic... but the wisdom from above is first pure, then peaceable..." (James 3:15,17).

As we grow spiritually, we become less dependent on ourselves and more on God. This serves as our protection. When we give in to the flesh, we open ourselves to the enemy's influence. The real battle begins in the mind. Revelation—spiritual insight—starts there.

John said, "He must increase, and I must decrease." The same principle applies to us. The Spirit gives life; the flesh profits nothing. The words of Christ are spirit and life (John 6:63).

The revelation of His word is the first step to gaining access. Sometimes, you read a passage multiple times and feel it calling to you, even though its true meaning seems hard to grasp. This is often the Spirit guiding you into deeper understanding. It could be instruction, comfort, prophecy, or even rebuke. However, revelation must go through a mental gateway—our natural awareness—so that the Spirit can confirm the truth.

The Word grants the Spirit access to our minds. It is not that He lacks power, but we lack recognition. Revelation depends on spiritual awareness, not just reading skills. The childlike conscience, though innocent, becomes vulnerable when it starts to tell right from wrong. That awareness brings both temptation and faith. It offers the opportunity for confession and salvation, but also the risk of sin entering.

Romans 10:8-10 reminds us that the Word is near, on our lips, and in our hearts. First, for confession unto salvation; and now, for prayer through faith. This is the continuation of obedience to truth. From this place of spiritual fervor, prayer becomes effective because it is born of faith and driven by grace.

Grace allows us to choose righteousness and fulfill God's will. The law provides illumination, but our choices are not random; they are influenced by desire, whether it is fleshly lust or spiritual hunger. Paul said, "I had not known lust except the law had said, 'Thou shalt not covet.'" Sin takes advantage of the commandment through the desires of our flesh to provoke disobedience. However, we have not received a spirit of bondage again to fear, but the Spirit of adoption, by which we cry, "Abba, Father." This cry is not just verbal but a transformative expression from the standpoint of having the power to make a change. It is an unction, the voice of a heart changed by truth—a declaration of position and identity in Christ. It is faith made perfect in love.

Chapter 11

By what order or line of authority does the Body operate, and where do we fit into this order?

*"Ye also as lively stones, are built up a spiritual **house**, a holy priesthood, to offer up spiritual sacrifices acceptable to God by Jesus Christ." - 1 Peter 2:5*

The hierarchical view of the "line of authority" is insufficient to describe the proper order of the Church, but it is instructive in understanding spiritual authority. It resembles what the law did until the grace of Christ came. Although some leaders insist on a spiritual hierarchy to promote mandatory spiritual fatherhood and authority in ministry, this approach does not align with the teachings of the New Testament. The Apostles were part of the foundation, appointed by Christ, yet they remained members of the same body, with the same purpose as every other gift, for the edification of the Body. The line of authority is only relevant for the administration and function of the visible Church. However, as a new believer, I have heard many preachers emphasize the importance of finding your spiritual father or the necessity of a human spiritual head, claiming it is the model left by the Prophets and Apostles. Nonetheless, these positions were not intended to establish a hierarchy; instead, they served as representatives or messengers. The Prophets of the Old Testament were messengers of God, and the Apostles were the forerunners sent by Christ as pillars of His Church.

God is holy other than we are, and the apparent hierarchy within the Godhead of Father, Son, and Holy Spirit serves as a sufferable designation for our understanding of a Triune God. Regarding Christ and His Church, this is not a positional relationship but one of ownership; however, in this context, it is intimate, akin to being the owner of our body, the head of a household, the father of our children, and the bridegroom of the bride. In the glory of inheritance, we are called His bride, brethren, sons, and daughters.

When God called, He called us out of bondage and adopted us into sonship. Our gifts and offices are insignificant compared to our sonship in Christ. The positional significance of our gifts and offices in the Kingdom of God is akin to that of a servant in a natural household. If we are to lean on or boast in any title or position, it is solely in the fact that our names are written in the Lamb's Book of Life and that we are adopted as sons and daughters. Therefore, all are equal in the Body. The local churches are not a necessary structure of positions but a reflection of diversity in gifts and callings that mirrors the universal Body of Christ. Although not every instance is the same, in terms of relevance, contemporaneity, or history, we must reflect the orthodoxy of the Gospel. However, the enemy often exploits our misunderstandings to deceive and manipulate our conscience.

As a young believer, I was frustrated in my search for a spiritual father. Sometimes, I even felt condemned after hearing at least two sermons delivering stern warnings. There was a strong impression of its absolute and immediate necessity. However, my conviction back then and the fruits of its wisdom today proved that the seasons and times of isolation He had me in were purposeful for His exclusive influence. Some of my attempts to submit to spiritual authority in obedience to these teachings only led to frustration. Perhaps the misunderstanding was on my part, but it occurred to me, and it can also happen to others.

My point is that our connection to God does not come through man's hierarchy but through our union in truth.

"I will put my law in their mind and write it on their hearts. I will be their God, and they will be my people. No longer will they teach their neighbor, or say to one another, 'Know the LORD,' because they will all know me, from the least of them to the greatest," declared the LORD. Jeremiah 31:33,34.

From my experience, I can say that God called me into the wilderness and kept me there for a time. Although I fellowship and worship with congregations, I found myself spiritually hungry and yearning for true fellowship with God. During periods of isolation, away from the noise of religion, I discovered true intimacy with the Holy Spirit and His Word. Along with selected teachings, He made His will clearer to me.

The clarity is not solely a result of isolation, but rather the culmination of a process that concludes there. As an unbeliever, I was searching fruitlessly in the dark, ignorant and naive, lacking the means and skills to conform. This left me frustrated and displaced by choices that led me from one location to another, with long-term consequences. As a believer, those consequences and dysfunction followed me, as did my pattern of moving from place to place. This meant many different congregations, denominations, and schools of thought. However, on this side of salvation, the frustration and restlessness drove me to search for a recognizable truth, as of the Spirit that first called me. The obvious problem with multiple denominations and schools of thought is the stagnating effects of their varied dogmas. There is nothing wrong with many modes of expression and cultural differences, but the truth should transcend all that.

The day I first encountered the Holy Spirit, I experienced an undeniable recognition and surrender, marking the end of a desperate search. This recognition, manifest through His presence and Word, has since been my standard for truth.

"I will put my laws in your heart and in your mind," not the dictation of stagnant religion and human dogmas. I am not saying that the truth cannot be found among the denominations and congregations; on the contrary, the Church is the pillar of truth. The issue lies in the variety of dogmatic views and the contradictions among those who should be part of the same body. The truth is unilateral by nature, and we all must stand before God in the unity of that truth. With the various doctrines, we undermine the order of the body; this is where the recognition of order arises: united by truth in the same doctrine and gospel of salvation. Connected by a grid of the same faith (the same theology) and empowered by the same grace for the same purpose in love.

This is what Paul calls "love without dissimulation," or one might say, the truth made evident by its device: the union of love. This union serves as the natural instrument through which the body operates, the brotherhood of love, or the priestly order of Christ. He is the blessing of Abraham in Melchizedek, and we are the Israel of God, a holy Priesthood.

In all this, we are off task, and those who claim authority and eminence continue to sever the body by demanding loyalty to man. Scripture never demands loyalty, but commands love in unity.

The dilemma of the modern church is not necessarily heresy, factions, and unorthodoxy. Paul said, "For there must also be factions among you, so that those who are approved may have become evident among you." Instead, it is the multitude of dogmatic teachings and the role of relativism in their interpretation of scripture within the body. More relevant to the topic of this chapter is the misconstrued spiritual authority and structure of the body, which stems from the false interpretation and claiming of the gifts and offices of the Church. The primary misinterpretation and appropriation often occur regarding the gifts of the Apostle and Prophet.

Apostles
When speaking of the Apostles, we can only refer to Jesus' disciples, the twelve he personally hand-picked. Those who received a direct

mantle from Christ, including Paul. Moreover, the authoritative writings of those who wrote on their behalf, such as Mark and Luke. I cannot speak to the full relevance of the gift to the body today, except regarding administration, where it serves the same purpose as a pastor or Bishop. However, as those sent out as founders in the Church and the establishment of doctrine, in that sense, those who claim to be Prophets and Apostles today are false.

The gifts of direct human representation of Christ ended with the Apostles, and the Apostolic Fathers of the 1st and 2nd centuries were tasked with preserving the teachings and texts as disciples of the Apostles, to pass on orthodoxy and reflect a universal consensus in practice and record as the Church grew. As a hierarchy, the office of the apostle was only temporary as a direct representation of Christ until the full transmission of the New Testament Canon. Nevertheless, the apostolicity of the Church remains a necessary universal presence.

This brings me to the second function of their office: to establish doctrine, or more precisely, scripture. Therefore, I also mentioned Mark and Luke above. The doctrine of the Church was established through the transmission of scriptures by the Apostles, specifically the Gospels, the Epistles, and the Apocalypse (also known as Revelation). The rest of the teachings were given beforehand by the prophets of the Old Testament, from Moses to Malachi.

Prophets

The Prophets, as related to the prophetic office, were primarily individuals called by God in the Old Testament. The prophetic engine of the ages was for the foretelling of the coming Messiah and His future kingdom. John the Revelator can be added to this rank for the book of Revelation. Although the gift of prophecy remains relevant and active in the Body today, it is not intended as a roadmap or a glance into the future of the world or the Body of Christ; God has already revealed this through His word. The primary purpose of the gift today is to work in conjunction with what the Apostles established and the rest of the scriptures: To expound, encourage, and bring us back to sound doctrine. Moreover, to edify the body, both as individuals and as congregations. The remaining gifts today are largely in line with prophecy, serving to edify the Body as a whole, which, when united in faith, operates under the same authority and headship of Christ. The push for human headship is the residue of our old disease of pride and a lust for power. Where there is the weighing of thoughts and man's wisdom, there is always the construction of hierarchy and the need for human authority. However, as you can see from above, there is no need for the weighing of human reasoning to distinguish truth outside of scripture. That was already done and fulfilled in Christ; the only thing left to do is to live by it.

"the law was given by Moses; grace and truth comes by Jesus Christ."

A spiritual house

⁴And coming to Him as to a living stone which has been rejected by men, but is choice and precious in the sight of God, ⁵you also, as living stones, are being built up as a spiritual house for a holy priesthood, to offer up spiritual sacrifices acceptable to God through Jesus Christ. - 1 Peter 2:4,5

A House, as in the natural, is a designated place of residence. In this case, the One Spirit resides in many mobile and transitive houses. The concept of spiritual dwelling transcends natural space and time and, therefore, does not need a stationary or immutable structure, yet He remains constant and unchangeable. As movable stones, we are made alive, hewn, and built into a house with spiritual bricks. We adapt to an immutable Spirit as we pass through this temporary life. Contrary to the many individuals who pass through time, residing in one body, many spiritual houses provide a spiritual home, subject to time, for the One Spirit who transcends time, so that one day we may transcend time.

There is a misconception about God's residence and presence. Believers are repeatedly told that they have an audience with God because they come to "the house of God" or a particular event or ministering. I have heard it preached on many occasions (and exclusively taught) that we do not have access to God's manifested presence except by a designated individual or place. Singers perform in the name of worship, declaring that the environment they provide enables the presence of the believer's liberty.

The assembly of believers in adoration, offering solemn praise and worship, brings a specific weight of God's glory. However, this is the corporate effect of His true residence by the honor He placed in us, and we return that honor to Him by demonstrating that residence. The designated time and place are necessary, but not for the mystical notion of granting access by religious zeal. No, it is for the worship and expression of a corporate body and the proclamation of the gospel to unbelievers. Otherwise, as believers, the indwelling of the Holy Spirit grants us a personal audience with God through Christ.

Priesthood: This is no longer a representation or an office but an order. It is no longer a matter of lineage of succession but the entire body. As was Israel's original call, "A kingdom of priests." However, they rebelled in disbelief and told Moses, "You speak to God!". So, it was performed through covenantal lineage after Aaron's order. Now, we have an actual spiritual body in the high priest of Jesus Christ, after the order of Melchizedek, who offered a sacrifice for our eternal salvation once and for all. It is called a "holy priesthood," transcendent in nature, an actual spiritual house. There is no designation of a priestly garment or office, but rather of spiritual sacrifice.

Sacrifice: Our physical death or any other sacrifice no longer has any merit before God, except our spiritual lives, as we trust in Christ. "As living stones," our lives lived not unto death but unto life, as on a new timetable, quickened by the Spirit unto a new purpose.

"Acceptable to God" - The acceptable aspect here is not even ours. In a sense, God accepts nothing from us; everything is through Jesus; some translations say, "by Jesus Christ" or "through Jesus Christ." The only sacrifices accepted and offered to God are those made by Jesus

Christ. Anything acceptable indirectly, as from us, is (by faith) through Jesus Christ. This leaves us with a paradox. To be a <u>living</u> stone, our lives must be fitted into a spiritual house. As a holy priesthood, we can offer up acceptable sacrifices unto God, which we cannot do naturally.

My aim is not to shake any beliefs; in truth, by that paradox, we already have a guarantee in our <u>salvific choice</u> and eternal salvation, but it also needs to be true in our daily lives. The living aspect and the effects of its abounding grace are only valid if it is relative to this life. The mystery of the paradox is in your will, or rather, your obedience to God's will. The once and for all sacrifice that inaugurated this holy priesthood was consummated the same way, "not my will, but Thy will be done," in the garden of Gethsemane, where the hand of Rome was permitted to take hold of the Lord of glory.

I have been crucified with Christ; and it is no longer I who live, but Christ lives in me; and the life which I now live in the flesh I live by faith in the Son of God, who loved me and gave Himself up for me. - Galatians 2:20

Back to the house of God.

In the Old Covenant, God's primary concern was not a temple for Himself or the ark of the covenant. It was the heart of the people, and the cleanliness of their hands. For instance, He allowed His ark to fall into the hands of the uncircumcised and allowed it to remain outside the care of the priest until they got their act right. A man died presuming to be in place in the will of God when he stretched out his hand in goodwill to support the stumbling ark. David, through whom the Messianic throne was established, was refused permission to build the temple because his hands were stained with the blood of war. God does not care about our structural and physical assemblies if they are not the assembling of a spiritual house. It must be distinguished by the corporate consciousness, which is the body of Christ, rather than its sacerdotal nature or the power of an ordained priest. There is no set-apart individual in the human priesthood, as with Aaron. Therefore, our sacrifices bear no contrast between the laity and the clergy, but are a unilateral act by Christ as we abide in Him.

*"That the righteousness of the law might be fulfilled in us, **who walk not after the flesh, but after the Spirit**" -Romans 8:4*

(The human soul (mind, will, and emotions), responding from his renewed spiritual volition and inclinations rather than his carnal nature). This happens by grace and conviction.

"But he gives more grace."

Grace is God's position to man in Christ, as we oppose truth in the flesh. Its most relevant aspect of truth to our daily life, in sanctification, is conviction. It informs us of our level of obedience to God's will. However, conviction was only possible by Christ's sacrifice, being subject to death inherited in Man's will. In that, we got another opportunity to obey. Conviction is grace's judgment in God's mercy in the elect. It feels somewhat like separation anxiety or "the loss of a loved one" syndrome. God, in his grace and mercy, draws back from us like judgment under His presence or from anything unholy. It lets us know where we miss the mark, but this experiential loss of peace also brings real grief and the guilt of our sin. Yearning to restore the relationship, we come to a place of humility with a repentant heart. Conviction is incorruptible, is heard beyond the mute of ignorance, and does not get seared as sometimes happens with the human conscience. However, we must take the opportunity it affords us through grace, by exercising our will. Otherwise, a seared and overridden conscience can justify the will of the flesh and, by natural reason, forfeit the benefit of grace in the ability to hear the voice of truth. The goal is to transition from conviction and repentance to a daily yielding to the Spirit's desires in worshiping God. This sacrifice as worship to God is a *"spiritual sacrifice acceptable to God by Jesus Christ."*

Or do you think Scripture says without reason that he jealously longs for the spirit he has caused to dwell in us? But He gives more grace. That is why the scripture says: "God opposes the proud but shows favor to the humble." -James 4:5-7

Chapter 12

You Need to Yield to the Order Sacrificially

⁷Then come the day of unleavened bread when the Passover must be killed.

⁴¹And he was withdrawn from them about a stone's cast and kneeled down, and prayed saying, Father, if thou be willing, remove this cup from me: nevertheless, not my will, but thine, be done. -Luke 22:7,41

Jesus' death on the cross may never be comparable to our calling, but he was still fully human. Despite his humanity and natural inclination for self-preservation, he yielded to God's will sacrificially. As God called him, so He enabled and strengthened him to accomplish it. Jesus' surrendering in the garden, in prayer, was a culmination of his faith in God's will. Likewise, God confirmed the faithfulness of His word (beforehand), by the charge of His angels, strengthening and comforting him.

...And there appeared an angel unto him from heaven strengthening him.

Remember in Chapter Eight, "The Functioning of the Church," where I began to make the argument for the necessity of being in the body under apostolic order and being submissive. I used this scripture:

*"ye know that ye were Gentiles, carried away unto these dumb idols, even as ye were **led**."*

Although we may have gifts and a calling, we must still be subject to the body and its gifts for our growth and development until we can be led. In the meantime, we must learn through obedience until we come to the unity of the faith—a process of "Till 'a comprehension with all the saints." Moreover, at the end of Chapter Nine, "Your Function in the Church," James 4:5 asks; ...do you think that the scripture says in vain, The Spirit that dwelleth in us lusteth to envy (lust enviously)?" In other words, the Holy Spirit desires to have us as the world had us— immersed in and conformed to it, or rather, be transformed in our minds for the unity of the faith.

To come into the unity of the faith, Jesus did not need this process of "till" to overcome the rebellion we have against the Holy Spirit, as we do to overcome our natural rebellion, coming off being led by those dumb idols or demons. However, in his human nature, he had to be led. He showed us what it looks like and the dynamics concerning our call and faith.

In the same way Christ was led, from the beginning of his ministry, in the temptation in the wilderness, to His death on the cross, so we ought to be led. Whether through favorable or unfavorable circumstances, it did not determine his choices, but as comparable to the call on his life, so he was led.

*Then was Jesus **led** up of the Spirit into the wilderness to be tempted of the devil. And when he had fasted forty days and forty nights, he was afterward a hungry. And when the tempter came to him, he said, If thou be the Son of God, command that these stones be made bread. Then saith Jesus unto him, Get thee hence, Satan: for it is written, Thou shalt worship the Lord thy God, and him only shalt thou serve.*

Then the devil left him, and, behold, angels came and ministered unto him. - Matthew 4:1-3, 10-11 (KJV)

Led into the desert to be tempted by the devil after he had been fasting and weakened by hunger, he depended on the Word to overcome the enemy. Trusting in God, he learned not to yield against the pressure of temptation, and then the Angel of the Lord came and comforted him. This was in preparation for the submission to His call, which is the cross. The differences here in the processes are growth and the specific call. In the wilderness, when he was tempted, he used "as it is written," drawing reference to whatever the word says regarding that temptation.

But when that day came, he did not look for references against the evil that was about to come upon him, but he went to God and confirmed his call, "...*nevertheless not my will, but thine, be done.*

And there appeared an angel unto him from heaven strengthening him."

You may say, we cannot expect this level of confirmation and comfort in yielding to God, but I say we can. Speaking of the angels, Hebrews 1:14 says, *"Are they not all ministering spirits sent fort to minister for them who shall be heirs of salvation?"*

The sacrifice ends in Christ, or the sufficiency of sacrificially yielding or living ends with Christ's sacrifice; however, in a sense, it begins in the wilderness of this "till" process, where we learn to shed our idols and be led by that singular Voice. The reason this is so significant is that those other voices are resident in your natural inclinations. So, every time it calls, you must count it as dead and say, Not mine, but thine will be done.

This is the struggle vividly described in Romans 7. In 7:14, Paul says, *"We know that the law is spiritual; but I am unspiritual, sold as a slave to sin."* In the flesh, you have no choice but to serve sin under the law. Nevertheless, Paul says in 6:14,15,

For sin shall not be master over you, for you are not under law but under grace. What then? Shall we sin because we are not under law but under grace? May it never be!

We are under grace, not under sin, but the flesh remains in a struggle to sin. Furthermore, if we do not surrender our minds to the desire of sin, we honor grace instead of sin, and thus are not under sin. However, if we do sin, it should be seen as a battle within the mind that says, "What a wretched man I am!" rather than "I am under grace, therefore I can sin," while remaining fully aware of who I am in Christ and whom I serve. Essentially, it is a spiritual attitude, adversarial to sin, rather than an intellectual stance driven by fear of the consequences of sin.

This mindset is made evident and enforced when we go on the offensive with earnest prayer. It is only through prayer that you can honestly claim to be part of this ongoing struggle and have any confidence in truly serving God. Remember, in chapter ten, we stated that to truly engage by faith in the proportion to which we are called, Philippians 4:6 tells us that *"in everything by prayer and supplication with thanksgiving."*

It is serving God with your whole heart and soul, regardless of what is going on in the flesh, and also knowing that you are wretched and unmeritorious, irrespective of how well you are doing in the flesh, while acknowledging our victory in thanksgiving. We see this both in Philippians 4 and Romans 7:25, despite the despair of the flesh and wrestling in the mind

*"He condemned sin in the flesh, so that the righteousness of the law might be fulfilled in us, **who walk not after the flesh, but after the Spirit**"*

(The human soul (mind, will, and emotions), responding from a renewed spiritual volition and inclinations rather than his carnal nature; yielding your body to the desires of the Spirit).

In all, yielding to the body sacrificially ranges from the natural to the spiritual. We prioritize our life for the benefit of the Body, and it starts with Christ's sacrifice, which enables us to yield gracefully or by His grace. But the primary profession of our sacrifice is prayer and devotion to the Word.

"For those who are according to the flesh set their minds on the things of the flesh, but those who are according to the Spirit, the things of the Spirit."

Truth and Sacrifice

Through our observation and consideration, we come to understand individual personalities and show them love, often through selfless concern or a degree of self-sacrifice. However, true sacrifice requires intentional modeling and discipleship in the Word of truth, which sometimes calls for "unwilling" submission with obedience and trust.

In a healthy brotherhood, this encourages positive growth and develops into the fruits of rewards from the seeds of sacrifice. In turn, sacrifice is no longer hesitant but becomes a norm at the forefront and an offering made with joy.

Sacrifice becomes void when:

- Its objective is self-satisfaction apart from growth or profit to the body or family.
- Personal growth for profit, cost, or hinder the brotherhood or other individuals.
- It is blind or lazy zeal lacking knowledge, proper advice, or guidance.
- Not applied in knowledge, acknowledging the unchangeable law of the principles of truth.

Even when precautions are taken to avoid these pitfalls, misinterpretations driven by wrong motives or personal observations can cause our active consideration to become a potential source of scandal and offense.

Misinterpretation is generally rooted in misguided or wrongly applied truths or principles.

Truth taken out of context is detached from its source; therefore, it is no longer true.

The context of truth is the principle or law by which it functions. So, even if you hear the word and do not apply the law or principle behind it, whether physically or spiritually, you cannot walk in the revelation of truth.

The Word is three-dimensional: Doctrine, Principle, and Truth.

You stand on doctrine by faith, apply or activate the principle through obedience in hope, and walk in the truth by revelation.

The Word says in 1 Corinthians 13:2.

And though I have the gift of prophecy, and understand all mysteries, and all knowledge; and though I have all faith, so that I could remove mountains, and have not charity, I am nothing.

*Vs 13: And now **abide** faith, hope, and charity, these three; but the* greatest of these is charity (love; self-giving sacrifice).

Abides where? In truth.

Our active choices reveal our hope; whether life or death, regardless of whether we act in ignorance or knowledge. Whatever principle we follow will activate the law to reveal that truth.

The power of our choice extends beyond what we know and understand, depending on whether we make sacrifices or consider others selflessly. While our sacrificial choice can give our application wisdom and experience, it also creates a space for us in the realm of truth through revelation.

True sacrifice is a currency of redemptive power, but the value of a currency does not come from the bearer. It comes from the authority that issues (endorses or assigns value to) that currency.

The value of a true sacrifice is measured in life. Hence, a sacrifice is valid when it involves giving up something necessary, reversing the natural course, or depriving oneself of what is rightfully theirs in this life. As a result, through faith, when exercised, you activate the principle by the very act and share in Christ's sufferings—the same sacrifice that has redeemed us back to the authority of life, placing this authority at our power by faith. We just need to be willing to trust in this authority by yielding to it, which means participating in that sacrifice through faith.

As pertaining to the Body yielding sacrificially

- We must be built into that Spiritual house, and to do that, we need to escape the disillusionment caused by our current structural and organizational dysfunctions. By that, I mean it must truly be one house, unified by the corporate consciousness in Christ. Our willingness is the start of practical submission (local, parochial) to the Body or Order at large, sacrificially.

- As a structural function, the focus is on the local body, but as an operational function, the emphasis should be on the universal body. Therefore, we need to be aware of how the local body functions to serve and obey the universal or Spiritual Body.

In light of "A Spiritual house"

- We need to change our view from seeing local houses as separate entities to understanding them as members of the larger corporate body.

- We need to stop creating structure and order for the body or trying to rebuild what we believe to be the order and structure of the Kingdom. If we instead surrender to what has always been, God will reveal and instruct us on how He wants it reflected locally in the physical state of the Body of Christ.

- We need to stop framing doctrines and theology as mandates for human explanations beyond what God has revealed or illuminated.

- We must acknowledge that these are serious issues, or if those issues are minor, identify the parties and the source of factions based on evidence of division and moral disagreement within the Body.

- We are part of a Kingdom that tells us, "For our struggle is not against flesh and blood, but against the rulers, against the authorities, against the powers of this dark world and against the spiritual forces of evil in the heavenly realms" (Ephesians 6:12). However, we often try to develop religious strategies from a human perspective. We must at least operate from a spiritual perspective to put on "the full armor of God." Vs 13.

As we are part of the view and therefore subjective, we require an objective perspective. As I mentioned in earlier chapters, a truly objective viewpoint is to step into eternity and see from God's perspective. Because we do not have that normative, a theological gesture is granted to us through Christ by the spiritual gifts and the impartation of our divine calling. That is where our objectivity lies (when we surrender), given to us as God sovereignly wills; therefore, we remain submissive.

Religious leaders and "lords" of the faith take offense and criticize the boldness of claims of divine impartation made by those outside the spiritual elite or an approved school of thought. However, they accept by importing into the Body the theories, teachings, and psychoanalysis of intellectuals who only regard our transcendent and absolute truth with mockery.

Those who view the call of God as a rare privilege for a select few are often driven by ambition, titles, and status. This pride blinds them to the fact that there is no exception among individuals, only one exception in the Body from the world, and that worldly prominence is merely an outward sign of the gift. The body is gifted without regard to persons. Yes, it sometimes appears as if God favors some more than others, but consider this: this side of eternity does not provide a true view or measure of His glory. It may be the opposite—those who seem to experience greater favor may actually have a greater need for grace, to prevent falling into a destructive pit of pride and self-will.

Consider the principles of tithes and offerings, as well as appropriation.

- The original purpose and intent
- The contemporary argument from principle.
- The violation of the purpose defeats that principle.
- Undue burdens on the brethren for individual religious ambitions.
- Everyone who is called and receives a gift believes they are called to build a "ministry" and have a congregation.
- The saturation of leaders and pastors, with so few followers, is a clear indication of their misconception.
- The soliciting of the law and the need to build and maintain those ministries.

The argued justification is the principle of the tithe, and the contemporary interpretation is based on giving in faith. The current application of this faith often involves conveniently invoking the need to exercise it (e.g., the leader's necessity of a purchase), regardless of the follower's natural circumstances, sometimes at the expense of natural obligations and integrity. When we, the sheep, are commanded to such obedience of faith by obeying the voice of the 'shepherd,' it further demonstrates unwavering trust in God to provide, being excused by our motives, infancy, and ignorance in faith. God's grace may abound in our hearts' motives. However, everyone is responsible for learning His laws and principles for obedience and discernment.

I believe in God's goodness and favor; I certainly live by it daily, and He rewards our generosity generously. Still, He does not use the law as a rod to command our faith or invoke the principle of His blessings. Instead, the principle of the law is followed by faith, which allows us to trust Him and receive an inherent blessing.

The testimonies of our modern faith often serve more as psychological support than as supernatural rewards. Natural events that are not intentionally planned or recorded in our timeline, and which happen to align with current faith discussions, are often given a "faith" explanation.

- A sudden insurance payout for a past car accident is not a miracle from God.
- For those in need who are constantly burdened financially, receiving cash just in time to prevent disrupting their livelihood by meeting basic needs does not justify declaring God's manifested glory.

There is no doubt that he is involved in those claims, but in most such cases, it is for our protection from ignorance and destruction. Godly faith is not living on the edge of anxiety, waiting for daily provision to prove your trust; it is the peace that comes with security, whether in need or abundance.

Even under the law, when God called a man to build something, He never asked him to tailor the law to the people for provision but always provided. In some cases, through their faith and wisdom, they make the supernatural call evident.

In the early New Testament, faith was the mark of the call, and the proof of faith was demonstrated by the supernatural, not by quoting the law. Today, we are told we do not have faith if we disobey (the quoting of) the law, but those who instruct our faith by quoting the law cannot demonstrate the faith they claim to be called by.

The point is, if you are to lead and be imitated, there must be a mark beyond just human endurance, determination, and persuasion. Even my internal joy and conviction are more meaningful than religious zeal.

Ironically, every testimonial of faith today relates to money, medical issues (not even healing), and marriage, in which unbelievers tend to prosper more. In our carnality:

- Money is the primary human factor that controls and motivates worship.
- Dynastic aristocracy and capitalism are what substitute for the law and promises.
- Socialism was an overly simplistic attempt to deny true human nature.

The early church's communal purse was a practical way to suppress this competing influence of mammon on the human heart in worship.

The main purpose of the Acts recording was not to emphasize the principle of the tithe and offerings, nor to serve as a model for the modern church and its control over congregants' resources.

- The significance was more a reflection of the early church and the heart of the people.
- It served to remove the competition of mammon.
- It was the dwelling of the true Spiritual House and a reflection of true Spiritual sacrifice. The physical entity back then more proportionally represented the invisible Church.
- The moving from house to house reflected true fellowship and spiritual worship, and not a precedent or model for the modern church.
- The spiritual nature was reflected in the way resources were used: "He who gathered much did not have too much, and he who gathered little had no lack."

Modern denominations more clearly reflect a revival of aristocracy, a socialist version of mammon, and a return to Levitical law. Most of the modern church is both deceived and refuses to abandon the nature of the old heart of Ananias and Sapphira. Contrary to much of what is preached, the significance of their death was not over an offering (in most cases, the motive of this preaching is manipulation, and, inversely, it is the preacher who shares their guilt). I believe it is because they attempted to enter into spiritual worship through carnal means; it was the motive behind their giving and the lie itself, not a lack of generosity.

The authentication of the local Body

The value of the body must be seen through the individuals, as the entire body surpasses the walls of denominational and congregational principles, allowing for a local view of the body as a whole and an understanding of its true global nature, while maintaining the parochial structure intact. The individuals must be prioritized as members of the Body, not of the organization; yet, the organization must not suffer decay due to the actions of rebellious members. The organization's authenticity should be such that when a member is sick, it indicates the health of the body, with a discernible fix, rather than serving as an organizational priority with dispensable parts. Still, when rebellion comes from false or foreign attempts to assimilate into the body, it can be eradicated, not by crude judgment but by a discernible Spirit.

- C. S. Lewis, No.16 Screwtape letter, 2nd para.

   "The parochial organization, being a unity of place and not of likings, it brings people of different classes and psychology together in a kind of unity (God) desires. The congregational principle on the other hand, makes each church into a kind of club."

   "...the search for a suitable church makes the man a critic where" God "wants him to be a pupil."

This brings me to the dilemma of our modern cities: their unfriendly environment and impractical saturation of local organizations. It almost makes the parochial concept, in both theory and practice, outdated. If this is true, it would imply that God was caught unprepared by a technological blind spot.

Most of this clutter is caused by some genuinely misguided individuals, while others enter the body with an enterprise mindset.

The remaining issues come from inherent philosophical differences, specifically different schools of thought within the body.

The roots of this problem did not come from a corrupted source, but from self-absorbed shrubs that decided to franchise their bodies to their ideology and subclasses using the gift God gave them. This is where the body's sacrificial nature is essential for the bigger picture, by not marginalizing those who do not fit into your "class," but instead recognizing the gifts meant to promote growth for the entire body.

I doubt Luther, Calvin, Wesley, and the many others who contributed to the Body of Christ—through the Reformation, spiritual revival, and theological and doctrinal renewal—intended to create denominational offshoots. Nor would their contributions be the cause of so many factions if organizations objectively listened to the Holy Spirit's guidance when reading Scripture, instead of relying solely on human understanding. Each was gifted to help grow the body of Christ. It is our pride and ignorance that once again give the enemy a foothold in the camp. Paul addressed this issue in 1 Corinthians 1:12-17. Calvin also discussed it in his address to King Francis I of France, in his Institutes, and I am sure it has been debated many times since. In Paul's day, it was a straightforward issue, yet a technological blind spot did not hinder the Word; the approach remains the same.

Is Christ divided? Was Paul crucified for you? Or were you baptized in the name of Paul (Wesley, Calvin, or Luther)? It does not matter how prominent you are or how confident you are in your theological correctness. The fact that a faction claims our prominence sacrifices the unity of the Body. I am not saying to abandon the truth, but we all need to set aside our pride to restore the unity in truth. The representatives (including us), congregations, and denominations are not honorary titles; they are messengers of Christ. Each must recognize itself as part of or need to be connected to the universal body and be willing to give up its own prominence and accept orthodoxy, which, from our perspective, traces back to the early-century Apostolic teachings.

So, we should not immerse ourselves in schools of thought, but in unity of doctrine; nor the prominence of our division, but in the unity of the body; nor the prominence of our gift, but in the love of the brethren — not by ambition, but by commission.

Chapter 13

Yielding to Adequate Proportion in Service and Responsibility

Let two or three prophets speak, and let the others weigh what is said. If a revelation is made to another sitting there, let the other be silent. For you can all prophesy one by one, so that all may learn and all be encouraged, and the spirits of the prophets are subject to the prophets.
For God is not the author of confusion but of peace – as in all the Churches of the Saints. 1 Corinthians 14:29-33 (ESV)

In a personal recount, "Anger-The Demon Inside," I described my life as being held hostage by an ill temper until the Spirit of God rescued me. Through His grace, I was delivered from marijuana and other appetites. Yet, despite these victories, I continued to struggle with visceral episodes of anger. As I grew in sanctification, I remember two occasions when He placed me in situations that seemed to lead me into the proverbial wilderness. After failing those tests miserably (being provoked to obscenity) and returning home devastated, filled with shame and guilt, I asked God, "You delivered me from marijuana and took away other tastes and desires from me, but I have been begging you to take this anger from me. Why don't you?"

He said, "To the extent that you grow in love, to the extent you will be delivered (from this dysfunction)." This simple yet profound statement reframed my understanding: walking in deliverance from the bondages of the flesh is tied to our ability to grow and walk in love. The reign of God in our lives is not merely about exercising authority or discipline over external behaviors, but about the internal reign of His Spirit over our thoughts, desires, and motives. As we grow in the fruit of love, we learn to temper our natural tendencies and yield to the grace of His presence.

This is one half of the equation: the internal transformation and essential growth in sanctification. Although there is actual reign in our mortal bodies, there is also an invisible unity that shows the harmony among the Body of Christ to reflect our spiritual nature as members of His Kingdom.

However, as I initially wrote the chapter and read it, contemplating "Yielding to Adequate Proportion in Service and Responsibility," I realized that I understood what we needed to be and what the purpose and result should be. Still, I did not know how to achieve it.

I went to the main text, trying to decipher some profound truth, until I looked at the plain text. Then I realized that we spent so much time on the mysticism of our faith and the rest of the time trying to manipulate the Word, that we forgot the fundamental principle: to do what the Word says. 1 Corinthians 14:26 says, *"What then, brothers? When you come together (this is the church), each has a hymn, a lesson, a revelation, a tongue, or an interpretation. Let all things be done for building up."* It is as simple as it sounds: Do you have a hymn? Then, sing to edify the body. Maybe you have more than a hymn, but everyone else is singing. Common sense dictates it is the wrong time for tongues or prophecy, so you sing.

It may be an opportunity for tongues or prophecy, but will it benefit anyone? Is there an interpreter? If not, then keep it between you and God. Paul states that even when he prays in tongues, his spirit prays, but his mind is unfruitful. 1 Corinthians is so detailed in its instructions that it clearly distinguishes between what benefits our intellect and the regenerated soul, what builds up ourselves, and what builds up the church. *"The one who speaks in a tongue builds up himself; the one who prophesies builds up the church."*

Then he goes even further. He distinguishes the gifts based on their significance to believers and unbelievers. Verse 22 says, *"Thus tongues are a sign not for believers but for unbelievers,"* while prophecy is a sign not for unbelievers but for believers. Either way, he remains focused on the inside of the church. When an unbeliever enters the church, if they hear a group of people speaking gibberish, they will think they are crazy. *"But if all prophesy, and an unbeliever or outsider enters, he is convicted by all, he is called to account by all, the secrets of his heart are disclosed, and so, falling on his face, he will declare that God is among you."* 1 Corinthians 16:24,25.

Even if all prophecies are given, they should be delivered in an orderly manner during worship. Verse 27 continues, *"If any speak in a tongue, let there be only two or at the most three, and each in turn, and let someone interpret. But if there is no interpreter, let each of them be silent in the church and speak to himself and God."* The text is clear and concise, requiring no interpretation or deciphering. If there is no one to interpret the tongues, then they should be silent in the church. It is right there in the text. You ask, "What about Pentecost? Let us go to the text.

Act 2:5-6: *"Now there were dwelling in Jerusalem Jews, devout men from every nation under heaven. And at this sound the multitude came together, and they were bewildered because each one was hearing them speak in his own language."*

They served as interpreters. They said, "We hear them telling in our own tongues the mighty works of God."

As Paul mentions in 1 Corinthians 22-25, like prophecy, even the outsiders are convicted and called to account by all. He proved what the unbelievers would say when they heard them all speaking in tongues. Act 2:13: *"But others mocking said, 'They are filled with new wine.'"*

Contrary to popular belief and practice today, God never intended for us to sound or act as if we are out of our minds, nor is He a God of confusion.

Romans 12:5-8 says, *"So we, being many, are one body in Christ, and individual members of one another. Having then gifts differing according to the grace that is given to us, let us use them: if prophecy, let us prophesy in proportion to our faith; or ministry, let us use it in our ministering; he who teaches, in teaching; he who exhorts, in exhortation; he who gives, with liberty; he who leads, with diligence; he who shows mercy, with cheerfulness."*

As I mentioned earlier, exercising those gifts does not have to be a mystical journey, nor do they have to be a burden of religious zeal. We are gifted according to the grace given to us, and this gift is based on our ability to act. If you are financially strained, then it may not be in His grace to give liberally; however, if your gift is prophecy, the measure of your faith is guided by 1 Corinthians 14, and it should not entail decreeing over everyone's life.

This is where the true demonstration of God's reign begins—when we yield not only to law or principle but to the transformative power of grace and the foundational teachings of His Word, which enable us to walk in unity and love. His reign is more than a doctrinal rule or moral guideline; it is a living, breathing presence within our souls. As infirmities and character flaws submit to His Spirit, we are called to reflect that reign outwardly in our relationships with others and the greater Body of Christ.

The Spiritual Reign and the Unity of the Body
The reign of God within us manifests in unity among believers, expressed through genuine love. Romans 12:9 urges, *"Let love be without dissimulation. Abhor that which is evil; cleave to that which is good."* Authentic love must not be pretentious or hypocritical. It cannot simply be something we force ourselves to show; it must come from a Spirit-led life of sacrifice and self-control.

The presence of unity in the Church reflects this spiritual reign. When believers are aligned in love, an invisible bond of unity connects us despite our differences. This unity, however, is not just a superficial peace. Sometimes, love requires brutal truths and firm boundaries; ultimately, it serves to distinguish, unite, and nourish the whole Body.

"For God is not the author of confusion, but of peace, as in all the churches of the saints." (1 Corinthians 14:33)

Here, Paul emphasizes that the unity of the Church, rooted in love and guided by the Spirit, is intended to reflect peace and order among all congregations. This peace is not merely the absence of conflict, but a profound spiritual harmony that arises when everyone utilizes their gifts and fulfills their roles in love, without pretense or pretension.

Love: The Binding Force in the Body of Christ

Love serves as the adhesive that unifies the Body of Christ. The spiritual gifts manifested through the Holy Spirit are essential for the health and function of the Church, but without love, those gifts become meaningless or even detrimental. As Paul illustrates in 1 Corinthians 13, love is the foundation upon which all gifts should operate because love guides us toward the true purpose of those gifts, the edification and unity of the Church.

This love, however, must reach beyond individual congregations. While local congregations are essential, the Body of Christ is not limited to any single denomination or fellowship. The unity Paul speaks of spans all congregations of believers. Therefore, dissimulation—lack of genuine love—harms the larger Church, not just individual assemblies. It does not matter whether the toes are healthy if the leg is amputated.

True unity requires that the ascension gifts—apostles, prophets, evangelists, pastors, and teachers—operate in harmony throughout the broader Church to sustain unity in faith and purpose. "And he gave some, apostles; and some, prophets; and some, evangelists; and some, pastors, and teachers." (Ephesians 4:11)

The Growth of the Individual and the Body

We can trace the journey toward unity and love through a series of pivotal scriptures (Romans 12:1, 9, 10; 1 Corinthians 13; 14:32-33; Ephesians 4:11-13), each addressing different aspects of how the local congregation and the broader Body of Christ should function.

Romans 12:1, 9, and 10 emphasize the individual's sacrifice, urging believers to offer themselves as living sacrifices and to ensure their love is genuine toward one another. This leads to Paul's discussion in 1 Corinthians 13 about how love must undergird all spiritual gifts. Individual believers grow in love by exercising their gifts, but only when love is sincere can these gifts truly benefit others. Without love, gifts serve only to elevate individuals and, therefore, create division.

In 1 Corinthians 14:26-40, Paul explains how the gifts should operate in an orderly church. Mature believers must utilize their gifts in a manner that fosters unity within the local congregation. While love serves as the foundation, it is through the mature application of spiritual gifts that the body operates effectively, nurturing the unity of the broader Body of Christ.

The Role of Ascension Gifts in the Global Church

Ephesians 4:11-13 extends the principle of unity beyond the local congregation to encompass the entire Body of Christ. The "ascension gifts" are not solely intended for building individual congregations but are designed to establish a unified leadership across the global Church. As leaders, apostles, prophets, evangelists, pastors, and teachers must work together, guiding the Church toward the *"unity of the faith and of the knowledge of the Son of God, unto a perfect man"* (Ephesians 4:13).

The primary purpose of these gifts is administrative, ensuring that the entire Body of Christ grows in spiritual maturity and doctrinal unity. Leaders must not cling to their visions or agendas, as this can create schisms. Instead, they should foster a unified understanding of doctrine and practice throughout the Church. As Paul writes in 1

Corinthians 12:5, "There are differences of administrations, but the same Lord."

The Eternal Nature of Love

Ultimately, while spiritual gifts are essential for the functioning of the Church, they are temporary and meant for the present age. Love, however, is eternal. Though gifts like prophecy and tongues will ultimately cease, love will persist both in this life and in eternity. "Love never fails; but if there are gifts of prophecy, they will be done away" (1 Corinthians 13:8). Therefore, we must "covet earnestly the best gifts: and yet show I unto you a more excellent way" (1 Corinthians 12:31).

Love is the anchor that connects us to eternity, even as we exist in this temporal world. Through love, we reflect on and showcase the victory already achieved in Christ. This victory, while partially realized through the function of spiritual gifts, is ultimately fulfilled through the unifying and eternal essence of love.

Chapter 14

Worship in Spirit and Truth: A Reflection on True Worship

John 4:22-24 provides a profound insight into the nature of worship. Jesus' conversation with the Samaritan woman at the well highlights the distinction between ignorant worship and the true worship that God seeks.

"You worship what you do not know; we worship what we know, for salvation is from the Jews. But the hour is coming, and is now here, when the true worshipers will worship the Father in spirit and truth, for the Father is seeking such people to worship him. God is spirit, and those who worship him must worship in spirit and truth."

This passage reflects essential criteria for true worship, echoing themes found throughout Scripture, particularly in 2 Peter 1 and 1 Corinthians 14.

Criteria for True Worship

Salvation as the Foundation: Worship Begins with Salvation. Jesus' words reflect the necessity of being called to worship: "Except you are born of the water and the Spirit, you cannot see the Kingdom of

Heaven" (John 3:5). True worship flows from the transformative experience of salvation. Worship is not a right everyone assumes; it is an honor God bestows upon those He has called or born again.

Revelatory Knowledge (Epignosis): Worship must stem from a deep, revelatory knowledge of God. This goes beyond mere intellectual agreement; it includes experiential and transformative elements. As we deepen our relationship with God, our worship blossoms. Paul prays for the Ephesians that they may receive "the Spirit of wisdom and revelation in the knowledge of Him" (Ephesians 1:17). Such knowledge transforms worship from a ritualistic experience into a genuine, intimate connection.

Intellectual Knowledge: While worship engages the spirit, it also demands the mind. "I will sing praise with my spirit, but I will sing with my mind also" (1 Corinthians 14:15). Worship requires an understanding of God that is rooted in Scripture and the gospel. This knowledge does not have to be scholarly, but it should be founded on a reasonable comprehension of who God is and what He has done.

Edification and Conviction: Corporate worship must edify believers and convict the hearts of unbelievers. "But if all prophesy, and an unbeliever or outsider enters, he is convicted by all" (1 Corinthians 14:24-25). Worship should reflect the presence of God, prompting everyone present to recognize His sovereignty and authority.

Order and Reverence: Worship must be orderly and free from confusion. "For God is not a God of confusion but of peace" (1 Corinthians 14:33). Reverence and fear of the Lord should characterize every aspect of worship. Disorder, whether through chaotic expressions or disjointed practices, detracts from the holiness of worship.

The Day of Worship: Lord's Day or Sabbath?

The early Church, adhering to apostolic tradition, set aside the first day of the week for worship, commemorating Jesus' resurrection. *"On the first day of the week, when we were gathered together to break bread"* (Acts 20:7). While some advocate for observing the seventh-day Sabbath, the New Testament depicts the Old Covenant Sabbath as a foreshadowing of Christ. Paul writes, *"These are a shadow of the things to come, but the substance belongs to Christ"* (Colossians 2:17).

Worship is not limited to a specific day or place; rather, it is a continual offering of reverence to God. However, corporate worship holds a sacred priority and should not be taken lightly.

Violations of Worship in the Modern Church

Secular Intrusions: Worship services often intertwine with secular events, undermining the sanctity of the time dedicated to God. While hosting political figures, social advocates, or community events in the church can be important, these activities should not occur during Sunday service. Although these elements are beneficial, they should never overshadow the act of worship.

Entertainment and Personality Cults: Modern pulpits often prioritize talent and personalities, emphasizing entertainment over the proclamation of the gospel. This diminishes worship to a performance, shifting the focus from God to man. Preaching must return to its rightful place—exalting Christ and edifying the body.

Emotional Manipulation: Emotionalism often overshadows genuine spiritual worship. While worship can evoke deep emotions, leaders sometimes manipulate congregations to produce outward displays of fervor, equating volume and enthusiasm with spirituality. True worship allows for diverse expressions. Some respond with quiet awe, while others engage in joyful songs. Forcing conformity stifles authentic worship.

Prayer and Financial Manipulation

Corporate prayer often reflects performance, with elaborate sessions designed for financial gain or deliverance. Prayer for healing and provision is biblical, but the practice of linking financial contributions to blessings distorts worship. "God loves a cheerful giver" (2 Corinthians 9:7), but giving should not be coerced or connected to manipulative promises.

Glossolalia (Speaking in Tongues)

Tongues hold a place in the New Testament Church but are often misapplied, as I explained in chapter 13. Paul clearly states, "I would rather speak five words with my mind than ten thousand in a tongue" (1 Corinthians 14:19). Tongues without interpretation are unedifying in corporate worship. Additionally, the Spirit's fullness is not demonstrated solely by tongues, but also by love, joy, peace, and self-control (Galatians 5:22-23).

I have personally experienced the danger of trying to manufacture spiritual gifts – a minister at an altar expressing his frustration when I fail to speak in tongues as proof of being filled with the Spirit. The Holy Spirit is sovereign and cannot be manipulated. Attempts to "teach" tongues undermine the Spirit's role in bestowing gifts as He wills (1 Corinthians 12:11).

True worship is rooted in salvation, shaped by knowledge, and characterized by order and reverence. The Church must reclaim the sacredness of worship, ensuring that God remains the central focus of worship. As worshipers deepen their understanding and experience of God, they reflect His glory more profoundly, embodying the true worshipers the Father seeks.

Chapter 15

The Transcendence of the Church

Earlier in this book, we explored the mission of the Church and its functioning as individual members, the local body, and the universal Body of Christ. In Christ's prayer for His disciples in John 17:6-26, we see the early indications of this mission: A predetermined plan, structured and predestined in Christ Himself, and carried out by the Spirit of God. God entrusted Jesus with those who belonged to Him, and Jesus sanctified and commissioned them as apostles to reach the world from which they were chosen. This sanctification, however, was not confined to the Apostles; it continues through their writing to every generation of the Church, adhering to the exact words and teaching of Jesus: *"Neither pray I for these alone, but for them also who shall believe on me through their words."* John 17:20.

Paul echoes this in Ephesians 2:19-22, describing the Church as a household built on *"the foundation of the apostles and prophets, with Christ Jesus himself as the chief cornerstone"* (Verse 20).

Peter's Confession and Its Significance
"But who do you say that I am?" Simon Peter answered, *"You are the Christ, the Son of the living God."* And Jesus said to him, *"Blessed are*

you, Simon Bar-Jona, because flesh and blood did not reveal this to you, but My Father who is in heaven. I also say to you [this is who you are, born of this confession] *that you are Peter (Petros, a stone), and upon this rock (Petra, bedrock)* [the unfolding of this revelation], *I will build My church, and the gates of Hades* [the power of death] *will not overpower it. I will give you the keys of the kingdom of heaven,* [the authority of God's reign and authority] *and whatever you bind on earth shall have been bound in heaven, and whatever you loose on earth shall have been loosed in heaven"* [you will forbid or permit the actions and authority of the teaching and governance in the Church]. – Matthew 16:16-19

In Peter's confession, Jesus acknowledges Peter's blessedness in receiving this revelation. The use of Peter's name—Petros (meaning "a stone")—is significant because Jesus contrasts it with Petra (meaning "bedrock"), indicating that Peter's confession of Christ as revealed from Heaven is the foundation upon which the Church will be built. The "rock" represents the truth of Christ's identity as the Messiah and Son of God. This is the foundational truth that will sustain the Church across generations.

The Power and Authority of the Church

Jesus then declares that the Church, built on this rock of divine revelation, will be impervious to the "gates of Hades," symbolizing the powers of death and the forces of darkness. Empowered by Christ's authority, the Church will withstand these forces. This ensures the Church's invincibility against spiritual opposition, particularly the power of death, which Jesus ultimately conquers through His resurrection.

The Keys of the Kingdom

Christ further entrusts this inherited blessedness to the other apostles, as Peter did, and, by extension, the Church's apostolicity, with "the keys of the kingdom of heaven." This symbolizes the authority to govern, permit, and prohibit in matters concerning the reign of God. The authority to "bind and loose" is a rabbinical phrase referring to the power to make decisions regarding doctrine, discipline, and governance within the Church. Jesus further clarifies the exercise of this authority with an example of what to do if your brother sins against you, in Matthew 18:15-20. You go to your brother alone first; if he does not listen to you, you establish two or three witnesses to support your claim. This is to bear witness to the truth. However, if he still does not listen, the authority to declare judgment must come from the Church. By refusing to listen to the witnesses and the Church, he has already broken fellowship.

The text says, "Let him be to you as a gentile," and in Matthew 16:19 and 18:18, the literal translation says, "shall have been bound... shall have been loose." It indicates that it is already established in heaven and whatever action we take precedes from heaven, emphasizing the Church's role as an extension of God's authority and judgment. The Church is not a transient, man-made institution but a divinely ordained body, structured and predestined in Christ and fulfilled by the Spirit of God.

The Unifying Nature of the Church

No human institution, whether a university, hospital, or business, exists without a guiding vision or the qualifications of its founder. Once these standards are established, the organization functions within a shared framework of values and goals. Whether it is a capitalist venture striving for profit or an academic institution seeking accreditation, each relies on following a recognized system to ensure its future growth and legitimacy.

Similarly, the body of Christ, the Church, holds a proven vision validated by its Founder and grounded in an eternal and unshakable system. Christ established this foundation through His life, death, and resurrection, and His work is recognized and acknowledged across all nations and cultures. The Holy Spirit serves as the accrediting power, sealing believers and establishing the Church in every generation according to God's unchanging standard. This unifying force is rooted in Scripture and has been realized throughout history, demonstrating its legitimacy and continuity into the future.

This divine institution is not an abstract concept but a tangible and practical entity, just as real as any human organization. However, unlike human institutions, it has a spiritual origin governed by heavenly authority. As members of this body, we are called to reflect a unified faith anchored in Christ, empowered by the Holy Spirit, and demonstrated through love.

While believers may differ in format and practice, these differences should not weaken the unity of the Church. The variety of expressions within the body of Christ can coexist with the unifying foundation of faith. When our principles and motives align with Scripture, our outward expressions show a genuine relationship with God, characterized by peaceful communication among ourselves rather than just zeal without understanding. True unity is not about uniformity, but about the shared faith, hope, and love that define the Church.

Paul illustrates this idea in 1 Corinthians 13:13: "And now abides faith, hope, love, these three remain." These core virtues form the foundation of the Church, helping to bring believers together despite differences in doctrinal expression.

This unity of faith is foreshadowed in Israel's history, exemplified by God's covenant relationship with His people, beginning with Abraham, who showed faith by leaving his father's house to follow the one true God, trusting in God's promises and turning away from idolatry. Israel's hope during the Exodus from Egypt and their trust in God to lead them to the Promised Land represent the hope for a future inheritance as God's chosen people. God's love, demonstrated through the law's provisions for redemption—whether by kinsman redeemers, gleaning for the poor, or safeguarding family inheritance—embodies the charity or love that sustains the community.

The law was not a tool of oppression but a reminder of how far people had strayed from God's grace. Now, through Christ, we are rooted in grace, not law. The Holy Spirit, as our seal, unites us with the Father and the Son. However, despite this, divisions among us often reflect the failures of natural Israel. Doctrinal deviations can often hinder the truth of grace, leading us away from the simplicity of faith.

The Fragmentation of the Body

At the core of much division in the Church is not a split in faith but of doctrine. Many disagreements stem from sincere convictions, though misguided. As Paul said about Israel, "they have a zeal of God, but not according to knowledge." (Romans 10:2) However, we often cling to these personal preferences, causing rifts, while claiming that such differences neither qualify nor disqualify someone's faith. The irony is that when we first came to faith, we were united by simple belief in Christ. Yet, as we gained knowledge, these doctrinal differences became barriers of division instead of helping us grow in the faith.

The Church's witness to the world weakens when we focus on personal dogmas instead of the unity of love and God's grace. Our gospel message is effective not because of doctrinal pride but because of its purity—showing God's grace, love, and unity. As Paul says, "faith working through love" (Galatians 5:6) is the key to being a real witness.

Section 2

Church History and Orthodoxy

Human beings, driven by our motives and efforts, cannot be trusted to remain faithful to transcendent truths. Our inherent narcissism and narrow perspectives, despite our good intentions, consistently blind us with biases. We are often convinced that our viewpoint is always the correct one. Nevertheless, God has bestowed a measure of wisdom (a providence of truth) upon every generation, ensuring that He always has a witness, even if it comprises only a few who are obedient to His word. Therefore, by His grace, we may continually cultivate a progressive and contemporary understanding of truth. Every generation will witness this as He continues to illuminate His people with the same Spirit. In that light, what follows is not a comprehensive examination of the church's history but an exploration of some essential people, places, and events in the history of time and space that affirm the nature of the church in history—a context necessary for our theology.

Academic and popular historical records often fail to distinguish between orthodoxy and non-orthodoxy, particularly when natural forces of persuasion and power assert orthodoxy at various points in time. Meanwhile, the factions that proclaimed orthodoxy maintained core teachings and added or interpreted others to their benefit. History's responsibility is to be objective in its record, while truth remains in the hands of God, from which the branches of orthodoxy trace their origins to apostolic roots.

Chapter 16

The Apostolic Fathers and Literature

The Fathers (not the Apostles) continued to systematically apply Scripture across episcopacies (church governance and bishoprics) through their teachings, literature, and scholarly interpretations, modeling literal applications based on apostolic tradition. Today, we debate whether Scripture should be taken literally, but in the past, instructions were followed literally, as evidenced by early Church literature. The Fathers are fallible; while they embody a line of apostolic and traditional orthodoxy, they also import their zeal and predisposed convictions. Passion and conviction can sometimes surpass general authority but often serve valuable purposes. When insufficient or incongruent, these, though reliable anchors of our apostolic traditions, must yield to the faithful instructions and interpretation of Scriptures.

The Didache

The Didache, also known as "The Teaching of the Twelve Apostles," is one of the earliest Christian writings outside the New Testament. It serves as a practical guide for Christian living, community organization, and worship. Here is a brief overview of its sixteen chapters:

1. The Two Ways; The First Commandment: This chapter outlines the paths of life and death, emphasizing the first commandment to love God and your neighbor.
2. The Second Commandment: Gross Sin Forbidden: This chapter outlines commandments against various gross sins, highlighting the importance of ethical behavior.
3. Other Sins Forbidden: This section continues to enumerate sins to avoid, addressing more specific actions and attitudes.
4. Various Precepts: It provides practical advice on daily living, including how to treat others and how to conduct oneself.
5. The Way of Death: This section explores behaviors and attitudes leading to spiritual death, contrasting them with the path of life.
6. Against False Teachers and Food Offered to Idols: This section warns against false teachers and offers guidance on handling food sacrificed to idols.
7. Concerning Baptism: This section provides guidelines for performing baptisms.
8. Concerning Fasting and Prayer (The Lord's Prayer): It recommends practices for fasting and prayer, including the Lord's Prayer.
9. The Thanksgiving (Eucharist): This section gives guidance on celebrating the Eucharist, also known as Thanksgiving.
10. Prayer After Communion: This section suggests prayers to be recited after receiving Communion.
11. Concerning Teachers, Apostles, and Prophets: It discusses how to identify and engage with teachers, apostles, and prophets.
12. Reception of Christians: This section guides how to welcome and support traveling Christians.
13. Support of Prophets: This section emphasizes the importance of supporting prophets.
14. Christian Assembly on the Lord's Day: This section provides instructions for gathering on the Lord's Day, commonly referred to as Sunday.

15. Bishops and Deacons; Christian Reproof: It offers guidelines for appointing bishops and deacons and administering reproof.
16. Watchfulness; The Coming of the Lord: This section encourages vigilance and preparedness for the second coming of Christ.

The Didache provides valuable insights into early Christian practices and beliefs, emphasizing the importance of living a righteous life, supporting community leaders, and being watchful for Christ's return. However, Roman Catholic and modern religious scholars argue that the Didache and other apocryphal texts are sacred writings, backing the narrative of their papal succession and authority from Peter. They contend that after Peter's death, Christians needed to form an organized movement to survive, and the Didache served as the main guide for establishing the Church. They also assert that, without a Bible at the time to teach them faith and practices, the Didache filled that essential role.

The premise is that the Church's function relied on Peter's leadership; consequently, its survival depended on that succession and the formal organization. However, as you will see in the section on Canon and elsewhere throughout this book, it is clearly stated in Scripture. The foundation and structure of the Church are based on the Apostles, and authoritative documents, such as the Epistles, which are declared to be scripture, provide instructions and a system of governance for the Church.

However, as early as this writing, it is evident that they began to expand upon the simple instructions of the Bible, marking the start of traditions that include additional requirements alongside scripture, such as specific liturgical formulas (e.g., fasting before baptism, water temperature, etc.), detailed ritual requirements, and the development of a hierarchical structure.

Barnabas (Died 61 AD)

Barnabas played a vital role in the early Church by sharing the gospel, especially with the Gentiles. Here is an overview of his contributions and viewpoints.

- **Advocacy for Paul:** After Saul's conversion, Barnabas vouched for him in Jerusalem, helping him join the community despite initial fears and suspicions (Acts 9:20-30). Barnabas recognized Saul's calling and brought him from Tarsus to Antioch, where they served together (Acts 11:25-26).
- **Mission to the Gentiles:** The church in Jerusalem sent him to Antioch to minister to the new believers there (Acts 11:22). He collaborated with Paul to teach and spread the Gospel, making significant contributions to the early church's outreach to Gentiles.
- **Leadership and Encouragement:** Known for his supportive nature, Barnabas played a crucial role in establishing early Christian communities and helping new believers. He was influential in the Antioch church, where believers were first called Christians (Acts 11:26).

Letter of Barnabas

The Letter of Barnabas, although not considered part of the canonical scriptures, offers valuable insights into early Christian beliefs, particularly regarding the relationship between Judaism and Christianity. In "Chapter 2: Jewish Sacrifices Abolished," Barnabas states that Jewish sacrifices and rituals were abolished with the coming of Jesus Christ, who established a new covenant. He emphasizes spiritual worship over physical sacrifices, referencing prophetic critiques of ritual offerings (e.g., Isaiah 1:11-14). The letter encourages Christians to seek wisdom, understanding, and knowledge through faith, patience, and purity.

Theological Context

Barnabas's perspectives highlight a broader theological conflict in early Christianity.

- **Conflict with Judaizers:** Judaizers argued that Gentile converts must adhere to Jewish laws, including circumcision and dietary rules. Barnabas, along with Paul, opposed this, championing the freedom of Gentile Christians from the legalistic demands of the old covenant (Galatians 2:1-10).

- **Typology and Prophecy:** Barnabas used typology, seeing Old Testament laws and rituals as foreshadowing Christ's work and the new covenant. He aimed to show how prophecy is fulfilled in Jesus, highlighting the spiritual meaning of the Mosaic Law.

Barnabas' writings might seem to contain anti-Jewish sentiments, but it is crucial to understand them within the context of religious debate rather than ethnic bias. The tension was primarily religious, focusing on how scripture is interpreted and its fulfillment in Christ. He criticized the Judaizers' emphasis on old covenant practices, not the Jewish people as an ethnicity. Developing the Christian identity, early Christians, including Barnabas, separated their faith from Judaism while remaining grounded in the Scriptures. This often involved discussions against Jewish practices seen as incompatible with the new covenant. Barnabas's work was crucial to the early church's growth and theology, particularly in defining a distinct Christian identity that welcomed Gentiles without requiring adherence to Jewish law.

Hermas (ca. 155)

The Shepherd of Hermas was valued for its practical advice and spiritual insights. It is often grouped with the Didache and the Letter of Barnabas. Although it is not part of the official Scriptures, it was popular in the early church for its moral lessons and guidance on living a Christian life. It was primarily used to teach catechumens—new converts preparing for baptism.

Similitude 5 – Of True Fasting and Its Reward

Chapter 1 Excerpt:

- "...You do not know," he says, "how to fast unto the Lord: this useless fasting which you observe to Him is of no value." "Why, sir," I answered, "do you say this?" "I say to you," he continued, "that the fasting which you think you observe is not a fasting. But I will teach you what is a full and acceptable fasting to the Lord. Listen," he continued: "God does not desire such an empty fasting. For fasting to God in this way you will do nothing for a righteous life; but offer to God a fasting of the following kind: Do no evil in your life and serve the Lord with a pure heart: keep His commandments, walk in His precepts, and let no evil desire arise in your heart; and believe in God. If you do these things, and fear Him, and abstain from every evil thing, you will live unto God; and if you do these things, you will keep a great fast, and one acceptable before God."

My Reflection on Fasting

I especially like this one because I can relate to it. Ritual fasting has always felt empty to me, and it became clearer as I experienced the true benefits and unselfish motives of fasting when guided by the Holy Spirit. I recall that, as a young believer, I got sick after fasting out of pure zeal. When I asked the Lord why, He convicted me, "I never told you to fast." Since then, my fasting has been rare compared to our traditional customs, but it has become more meaningful and instructive, like during a five-day fast from food, an experience I will share with you in Volume 2. I realized that, although these practices are good habits for piety, they are most effective when led by the Spirit to achieve specific results according to God's will: to subdue the flesh in obedience and to help answer prayers. For example, the five-day fast from food reset my taste buds and changed my entire diet, which was prompted by prayer for physical health and mental clarity. This resulted in impressive outcomes, including a radical shift in my food preferences, improved physical health, emotional stability, mental focus, and drive. My closeness to God has only grown as I serve Him with a pure heart (not out of guilt), follow His instructions, and believe in Him. This is the true fast that is acceptable to God, as Hermas emphasizes. So yes, my experience with fasting resonates deeply with the teachings in The Shepherd of Hermas.

Key points to consider

1. **True Fasting vs. Ritual Fasting:** Hermas highlights that true fasting is not just about skipping food; it is about living rightly, serving God sincerely, and following His commandments. By grasping this, effective fasting enables us to become more receptive to the Holy Spirit, rather than just going through an empty ritual.

2. **Spiritual and Practical Benefits:** Fasting with the right motives and following God's guidance also brings natural benefits, such as better physical health, emotional stability, and improved mental focus. Hermas also states that true fasting results in living for God, which includes these holistic benefits.

3. **Guidance from the Holy Spirit**: Following God's instructions on when and how to fast is crucial. The story I shared about falling ill from fasting out of zeal and then being convicted by the Holy Spirit — "I never told you to fast" — highlights the importance of discernment and obedience in spiritual practices. This aligns with Hermas' teaching that acceptable fasting involves aligning oneself with God's will and living a pure, obedient life.

Insight on Fasting

Be intentional. Approach fasting with a clear purpose and divine guidance to ensure it is spiritually meaningful rather than just a ritual. Take an integrated approach. Recognize that true fasting involves abstaining from evil, serving God with a pure heart, and living by God's commandments. Fasting acts as a tool for spiritual growth, helping us get closer to God and experience transformation in our physical, emotional, and mental lives. By applying these principles, fasting becomes a meaningful and powerful practice that enhances our spiritual journey and aligns with teachings from early Christian writings, such as the Shepherd of Hermas.

Clement of Rome (35 – 99 AD)

Clement of Rome wrote influential letters that guided and resonated with the early Church. His first letter, often called the First Epistle of

Clement, is especially valued for its insights into faith, repentance, and the Christian way of life.

Key Excerpts from the First Letter of Clement

Chapter 7: An Exhortation to Repentance:

"...Let us look steadfastly to the blood of Christ and see how precious that blood is to God, which, having been shed for our salvation, has set the grace of repentance before the whole world. Let us turn to every age that has passed and learn that, from generation to generation, the Lord has granted a place of repentance to all such as would be converted unto Him. Noah preached repentance, and as many as listened to him were saved. Jonah proclaimed destruction to the Ninevites; but they, repenting of their sins, propitiated God by prayer and obtained salvation, although they were aliens (to the covenant) of God."

Chapter 8: Continuation:

"The ministers of the grace of God have, by the Holy Spirit, spoken of repentance; and the Lord of all things has Himself declared with an oath regarding it, 'As I live, says the Lord, I desire not the death of the sinner, but rather his repentance,' adding, moreover, this gracious declaration, 'Repent, O house of Israel, of your iniquity. Say to the children of My people, 'Though your sins reach from earth to heaven, and though they (are) redder than scarlet and blacker than sackcloth, yet if you turn to Me with all your heart and say, Father! I will listen to you as a holy people.' And in another place, He speaks thus: 'Wash and become clean; put away the wickedness of your souls from before My eyes; cease from your evil ways and learn to do well; seek out judgment, deliver the oppressed, judge the fatherless, and see that justice is done to the widow; and come, let us reason together. He declares, Though your sins be like crimson, I will make them white as snow; though they be like scarlet, I will whiten them like wool. If you are willing and listen to Me, you shall eat the good things of the earth; but if you refuse and will not listen to Me, the sword shall devour you, for the mouth of the Lord has spoken these things.' Desiring, therefore, that all His beloved should be partakers of repentance. He has, by His almighty *will, established these declarations. So let us yield obedience to His excellent and glorious will and imploring His mercy and loving-kindness, while we forsake all fruitless labors and strife and envy which leads to death, let us turn and lay aside every evil deed, emulating His practice and let us look steadfastly to the blood of Christ and see how precious that blood is to God, which having been shed for our salvation, has set the grace of repentance before the whole world."*

Themes and Insights

- Centrality of Christ's Sacrifice: Clement emphasizes the significance of Christ's blood, shed for salvation, as the foundation for repentance. This highlights the early Christian understanding of atonement and redemption.
- Historical Examples of Repentance: By citing Noah and the Ninevites, Clement illustrates the continuity of God's call to repentance throughout history. These examples remind believers of the enduring nature of God's mercy.
- God's Desire for Repentance: Clement quotes God's declarations, emphasizing that God does not desire the death of sinners but rather their repentance. This underscores the compassionate and forgiving nature of God.
- Call to Holiness: The appeal to "wash and become clean" and to cease from evil ways reflects a call for personal holiness and ethical living, which are integral to the Christian faith.
- Obedience and Emulation of Christ: Clement encourages believers to emulate Christ by forsaking strife, envy, and evil deeds, and to follow God's will, demonstrating the transformative effects of true repentance on one's life.

Application to Modern Christian Life

We apply those insights on repentance in several ways:

- Deep Reflection on Christ's Sacrifice: Understanding the depth of Christ's sacrifice can inspire a deeper sense of gratitude and a desire for genuine repentance.

- Learning from Biblical Examples: Reflecting on historical examples of repentance can provide encouragement and hope for personal transformation.
- Embracing God's Mercy: Recognizing God's desire for repentance and willingness to forgive us can foster a more compassionate and merciful attitude toward ourselves and others.
- Pursuing Holiness: Striving for personal holiness and ethical living in alignment with God's commands can lead to a more fulfilling and righteous life.
- Living Out Repentance: Emulating Christ and seeking to live out repentance in daily actions can lead to a more authentic and impactful Christian witness.

By incorporating these teachings, modern believers can find inspiration and guidance for a life of faith, repentance, and devotion, deeply rooted in the early Christian tradition.

The **Grace** of repentance is not always that which accompanies our modern repentance, a repentance of our intrinsic remorse. No, this is the gift of God, not of our own; an extrinsic judgement of guilt and rescue unto repentance accompanied with tears of joy–from faith unto faith.

"They love him with their mouth (zealous in religion) **and lied to Him with their tongue."** It was not a product of the heart and true repentance, but by will of the mouth.

Ignatius (ca. 35-108 AD)

The Bishop of Antioch, a zealous convert and disciple of John the Apostle, Ignatius was eventually captured by Roman authorities, sentenced to die in the amphitheater, and torn to pieces by beasts. On his journey from Antioch to Rome, he traveled through various cities, stopping to speak with fellow Christians and writing seven letters to six of the towns he visited. Ignatius emphasized doctrinal orthodoxy and provided strong encouragement to stay faithful, along with practical guidance on living and following the examples of Christ, the apostles, and the Old Testament Scriptures. He recognized that his upcoming death was an honor and privilege, joining the apostles and forefathers. His letters, sent to different Christian communities, provide valuable insights into early Christian beliefs and practices, emphasizing the importance of unity and doctrinal purity. The following two excerpts are from his letter to the Ephesians, which shows a humble plea for all the Churches to remain faithful to the Gospel.

Chapter 7: Beware of False Teachers:

"...For some are in the habit of carrying about the name (of Jesus Christ) in wicked guile while yet they practice things unworthy of God, whom you must avoid as you would wild beasts. For they are ravening dogs, who bite secretly, against whom you must be on your guard, inasmuch as they are men who can scarcely be cured. There is one Physician who is possessed both of flesh and spirit; both made and not made; God existing in flesh; true life in death; both of Mary and of God; first passible and then impassible, even Jesus Christ our Lord."

Chapter 8: Renewed Praise of the Ephesians:

"Let not anyone deceive you. As indeed you are not deceived, inasmuch as you are wholly devoted to God. For since there is no strife raging among you which might distress you, you must, of necessity, live according to God's will. I therefore exhort you to keep unity among yourselves, and to guard against those who would sow dissension and division among you. For there are some who would lead you astray by their false doctrines and deceptive practices. But you have not given them a hearing, and you must continue to reject their errors and hold fast to the truth which you have received. Let us therefore persevere in our faith and be zealous in doing good works, so that we may inherit the promises of God and attain to the joy of everlasting life."

Themes and Insights

- Warning Against False Teachers: Ignatius urges the Ephesians to stay alert against false teachers who claim to follow Christ but act unworthy. He highlights their danger by comparing them to wild animals and hungry dogs. This highlights the importance of exercising careful judgment and vigilance in upholding sound doctrine.

- Christ as the Divine Physician: Ignatius refers to Christ as the "one Physician" who embodies both flesh and spirit, both made and unmade, emphasizing the dual nature of Christ as both human and divine. This theological assertion highlights the mystery and significance of the Incarnation.
- Commendation and Encouragement for Unity: Ignatius praises the Ephesians for their devotion to God and their unity. He encourages them to preserve this harmony and be wary of those who might promote division through false doctrines and deceptive practices. He emphasizes that unity is vital for living according to God's will.
- Perseverance in Faith and Good Works: The call to persist in faith and diligently perform virtuous acts reflects Ignatius' focus on the practical expression of faith. He links this perseverance to the hope of inheriting God's promises and gaining eternal joy.

Application to Modern Christian Life
- Vigilance Against False Teachings: Modern believers can follow Ignatius's warning by carefully identifying teachings and practices that do not match the core principles of the Christian faith. This requires studying the Scriptures and seeking advice from trusted spiritual leaders.
- Embracing the fullness of Christ: Understanding and appreciating Christ's dual nature as both fully God and fully human can strengthen faith and enrich worship and devotion.
- Fostering unity in the church: Working toward unity within the Christian community, avoiding conflict, and rejecting divisive influences can strengthen the church's collective witness and help fulfill God's will.

- Commitment to Faith and Good Works: Staying dedicated to faith and actively practicing good deeds are essential for spiritual growth and showing Christ's love to the world. This involves serving others, advocating for justice, and living out Christ's teachings on a daily basis.

Ignatius' letters inspire and challenge believers to stay strong in their faith, keep unity, and live out their beliefs with honesty and dedication. His legacy as a zealous disciple and martyr highlights the transformative power of steadfast commitment to Christ.

Polycarp (69-155 AD)

Polycarp, Bishop of Smyrna and a disciple of John who ordained him, was loved and honored by congregations throughout Asia for his zeal and piety. He received letters of commendation from many faithful congregations. As the leader of the entire Church in Asia, he opposed Anicetus of Rome's desire to change the date of the Resurrection feast. Polycarp then returned to Asia, where he continued to teach and disciple his congregation.

Letter to the Philippians(excerpt):

Greeting

Polycarp, and the presbyters with him, to the Church of God sojourning at Philippi: Mercy to you, and peace from God Almighty, and from the Lord Jesus Christ, our Savior, be multiplied.

- Chapter 3. Expression of personal unworthiness

    These things, brethren, I write to you concerning righteousness, not because I take anything upon myself, but because you have invited me to do so. For neither I, nor any other such one, can come up to the wisdom (2 Peter 3:15) of the blessed and glorified Paul. He, when among you, accurately and steadfastly taught the word of truth in the presence of those who were then alive. ...

- Chapter 11. Expression of grief on account of Valens

    ... I am deeply grieved, therefore, brethren, for him (Valens) and his wife; to whom may the Lord grant true repentance! And be then moderate regarding this matter, and do not count such as enemies, 2 Thessalonians 3:15 but call them back as suffering and straying members, that you may save your whole body. For by so acting, you shall edify yourselves. 1 Corinthians 12:26.

This letter clearly shows that Polycarp, like the fatherly role Paul held over the Philippians (Ch. 3, par. 1), humbly exercises this privilege within the framework of Apostolic teachings and writings. He addresses every aspect of his message with references to their oral and written traditions, including the teachings of the fathers before him. Specifically, he refers to what is now known as the New Testament canons or scriptures. The situation discussed involves the fall of a brother named Valens, who also appears to be a presbyter. The tone of the address resembles Paul's approach in 2 Corinthians regarding the believer who was previously disciplined in 1 Corinthians. Polycarp uses this opportunity to encourage the saints in faith, virtue, and perseverance.

Another notable point is "Concerning the transmission of epistles," which was his response to the request from both the Philippians and Ignatius to circulate the epistles, especially those of Ignatius, whom they mutually knew. They also reminded each other of the usefulness of such letters. The absence of his text to us is no loss because everything in these letters is recitation or, at most, elaboration of what we now recognize as scriptures. However, as an important part of the generational bridge he helped create, Polycarp was among the first to endorse the distinction of the Apostle's writings as scripture.

Papias (ca. 70 – 160 AD):

"a hearer of John, and companion of Polycarp, a man of old time" - Irenaeus

A work of five books interpreting the gospels, *logion kyriakon exegesis*, of which just fragments are preserved.

- **A fragment(introduction) as recorded by Eusebius** (III. 39)

  "I will not hesitate to add also for you to my interpretations what I formerly learned with care from the Presbyters and have carefully stored in memory, giving assurance of its truth. For I did not take pleasure as the many do in those who speak much, but in those who teach what is true, nor in those who relate foreign precepts, but in those who relate the precepts which were given by the Lord to the faith and came down from the Truth itself. And also if any follower of the Presbyters happened to come, I would inquire for the sayings of the Presbyters, what Andrew said, or what Peter said, or what Philip or what Thomas or James or what John or Matthew or any other of the Lord's disciples, and for the things which other of the Lord's disciples, and for the things which Aristion and the Presbyter John, the disciples of the Lord, were saying. For I considered that I should not get so much advantage from matter in books as from the voice which yet lives and remains."

These writings were upheld by the churches of the time through apostolic tradition because they reflected the local expression of Jesus and the Apostles. They serve as guidelines for maintaining authority in church leadership and discipline. They affirm the validity and succession of authority and the proper responsibilities of the Fathers as they intervene and establish standards within their local regions. They were tasked with holding fast to the Apostles' doctrine and preparing the stage for the Apologetic Fathers to face the rising waves of opposition, such as Gnosticism, Monarchianism, and the various affluent schools of philosophy, polytheistic, and pagan religions.

Chapter 17

The Apologists

Regarding inquiries and questions about apologetics, my contemporaries have often explained that the term has no direct relation to how we typically use "apologize" or give an "apology" to acknowledge our fault. However, from my perspective, these terms are indeed related and share the same root. Originating from the Greek adjective "apologetikos" and carried over to the Latin "apologeticus," "apologia" serves as the firm basis for both the English "apology" and "defense." It possesses a dual nature, functioning as both a defense and an acknowledgment. A defense counters an attack, while an apology is an acknowledgment or retraction by the offender. They represent the justification of the accused by the accuser or the substantive defense of the just or innocent.

The Apologists gave the term its substantial nature, both defensively and offensively. They defended against verbal accusations concerning their livelihood, social and religious practices, and the Jews' rejection of the Messianic fulfillment. As the faith gained prominence, they had to engage with the intellectual and philosophical world. As a system growing within society, Christianity needed a coherent body of doctrine to convey its tenets and make a valid claim to the truth. This included developing a theological framework that adequately represented the faith.

A significant difference at that time was the physical attacks and legal edicts against Christianity, often punishable by death. Their defense appeared contradictory: defending the faith by not doing so themselves, willingly giving up their lives as martyrs. Today, "apologetics" has lost much of its original force, often taken up voluntarily or as a vocational option.

The Apologists primarily defended against external critics. However, as the church's body and intellectual culture grew, so did the distortions of truth and various heresies. Men with similar convictions, although sometimes holding significantly differing viewpoints, raised questions, provoked thought, and challenged the faith, leading to the strengthening of doctrines through a clearer understanding of truth.

Britannica notes that apologetics seeks to vindicate Christian theology through philosophical concepts such as logos—"the rational principle underlying and permeating reality" and "divine reason, incarnate in Jesus." The tension between the gospel and philosophy persisted throughout the patristic period, emphasizing that faith is both superior to and foundational for knowledge.

The Apologists engaged in battles against Jewish critics, a hostile pagan society, and increasing intellectual attacks, as well as distorted scripture and heresies from within. Some of the earliest, though less impactful, apologists include Quadratus (c. 101-150), Aristo of Pella, Apollinaris, Aristides, Athenagoras of Athens, Tatian, Theophilus of Antioch, Clement of Alexandria, Minucius Felix, Cyprian of Carthage, and Lactantius.

However, others have significantly shaped the doctrines that guard truth through generations, providing us with sound orthodoxy.

Justin Martyr (born early second century)

Justin's efforts in his First and Second Apologies, as well as his Dialogue with Trypho, illustrate his dual focus on addressing misunderstandings about Christian practices and engaging with Jewish conversers to demonstrate the fulfillment of Old Testament prophecies in Christ. His emphasis on rational investigation and justice over superstition and prejudice highlights the intellectual integrity he aimed to bring to Christian apologetics.

The First Apology: (Chapters I-LXVIII)

Excerpts -

- *Chapter II. —Justice demanded.*

    "Reason directs those who are truly pious and philosophical to honour and love only what is true, declining to follow traditional opinions, (Literally, "the opinions of the ancients.") if these be worthless. For not only does sound reason direct us to refuse the guidance of those who did or taught anything wrong, but it is incumbent on the lover of truth, by all means, and if death be threatened, even before his own life, to choose to do and say what is right. Do you, then, since ye are called pious and philosophers, guardians of justice and lovers of learning, give good heed, and hearken to my address; and if ye are indeed such, it will be manifested. For we have come, not to flatter you by this writing, nor please you by our address, but to beg that you pass judgment, after an accurate and searching investigation, not flattered by prejudice or by a desire of pleasing superstitious men, nor induced by irrational impulse or evil rumours which have long been prevalent, to give a decision which will prove to be against yourselves. For as for us, we reckon that no evil can be done us, unless we be convicted as evil-doers or be proved to be wicked men; and you, you can kill, but not hurt us."

- *Chapter LXV. – Administration of the Sacrament*

"... And when the president (the Brethren presiding) has given thanks, and all the people have expressed their assent, those who are called by us deacons give to each of those present to partake of the bread and wine mixed with water over which the thanksgiving was pronounced, and to those who are absent they carry away a portion."

There is a tone in this last excerpt that describes the early believers in a way that goes beyond our modern fellowship and worship. It is often reflected in our natural relationships, especially among "loved ones." "And to those who are absent, they carry away a portion." Although this was a shared act of faith, it also stemmed from an underlying value of affection. When you come home from a party and bring a little piece of cake for your significant other, or return from a trip with a special token for your son or daughter, it's not about the value of the item itself; it's a way of sharing the experience and showing that person they are important to you. It is rooted in love, not just a product of community or even domestic life.

The Second Apology: (Chapters I-XIV)
Excerpts –
- *Ch. IV. (Why Christians do not kill themselves).*

  "... We have been taught that God did not make the world aimlessly, but for the sake of the human race; and we have before stated that He takes pleasure in those who imitate His properties and is displeased with those that embrace what is worthless either in word or deed. ..."
- *Ch. VI. (Names of God and of Christ, their meaning and power).*

  "And His Son, who alone is properly called Son, the Word, who also was with Him and was begotten before the works,

when at first, He created and arranged all things by Him, is called Christ, in reference to His being anointed and God's ordering all things through Him; this name itself also containing an unknown significance; as also the appellation "God" is not a name, but an opinion implanted in the nature of men of a thing that can hardly be explained. But "Jesus," His name as Man and Savior, has also significance. ..."

- Ch. VII. (The world preserved for the sake of Christians. Man's responsibility).

    "Wherefore God delays causing the confusion and destruction of the whole world, by which the wicked angels and demons and men shall cease to exist, because of the seed of the Christians, who know that they are the cause of preservation in nature. ..."

Dialogue with Trypho: (Chapters I-CXLI)

This dialogue clarifies religious debates over Old Testament prophecies, demonstrating how Jewish laws, types, and shadows all pointed to Christ. It addresses scripture transcription and translation, helping orient our faith and resolve subtle debates.

Irenaeus of Lyon (c. 130-c. 202)

Irenaeus of Lyon's comprehensive work, Against Heresies, methodically dismantled Gnostic doctrines, safeguarding the early Church's orthodoxy. His emphasis on unity, particularly in the debate over the celebration of Easter, reflects his broader concern for maintaining the Church's cohesion in the face of divisive issues.

In his work, we learn that Irenaeus saw and heard Polycarp as a child. Born in Asia Minor to Greek parents, he became a priest and later the Bishop of Lyons after the martyrdom of Pothinus. He served as a missionary and mediator, particularly regarding the celebration of Easter. Irenaeus argued that external factors, such as dates, should not divide the church. He interceded on behalf of Asia Minor with Pope Victor concerning their excommunication over Easter celebrations. A methodical critic of Gnosticism, he provided a reasonable account of their doctrines and heresies.

Against Heresies:

Book I

Book II

Book III

Book IV

Book V

Fragments from the Lost Writings of Irenaeus(condensed)

"Error is never set forth in its naked deformity, lest it be detected. It is craftily dressed to appear true to the inexperienced. A clever imitation in glass casts contempt on a precious jewel unless examined by a skilled eye. Error appears in sheep's clothing, resembling our language but differing in sentiment. After reading some Commentaries of the disciples of Valentinus and understanding their tenets, I reveal these mysteries to help others avoid such madness and blasphemy against Christ."

Origen (c. 185-c. 254)

Despite some speculative errors, Origen's De Principiis illustrates his pioneering efforts in Christian thought. He grappled with complex theological concepts and aimed to articulate a coherent Christian worldview. Origen's works include De Principiis (On First Principles), Letters of Origen, and Origen Against Celsus (Contra Celsum). He led the prominent school of Alexandria. Regardless of his mistakes, Origen's work laid the foundation for future Christian theology. He engaged in speculation beyond scripture on topics such as the soul and eternity, but his contributions to orthodoxy are substantial.

Comment on *De Principiis:*

Book I, Chapter I: On God

Some argue that God is a body based on scripture passages describing Him as fire or spirit. However, passages like "God is light" indicate an influence of God illuminating understanding, as seen in "In Thy light we shall see light." This light represents divine wisdom, not physical light.

Tertullian of Carthage (c. 160 -c 220):

"What has Athens to do with Jerusalem?" he asked.

Born to a centurion in the African-based legion, he was educated in Carthage and continued his studies in Rome as a young adult, where he began his career as a lawyer. Tertullian became interested in Christianity in Rome, but converted to Christianity after returning to Carthage.

Tertullian was the first notable Latin theologian. He converted to Christianity, likely before but no later than 197. He was ordained a priest around 200 and held very strict moral views, so much so that in the later part of his life he joined the Montanist sect around 206, then distanced himself from the church between 211 and 213. He eventually founded his sect and separated from Montanism, presumably because they also fell short of his moral rigor. The remnants of his sect were later reconciled with the church by St. Augustine. Ironically, Tertullian was among those who rejected the idea of a merciful church but insisted on a church that is pure and free of sinners. He rejected the notion that the Church, as the pure bride of Christ, can extend forgiveness and repentance to the so-called "lapsed." These were Christians who denied Christ under threat of persecution and execution. This act of apostasy was considered one of the worst sins, alongside murder and adultery.

Like all true patriarchs, the margin of their pioneering errors does not diminish their contribution to the development of the Church's theology. His writings and engagement with faith defended, promoted, and preserved the gospel; helped normalize the use of text as orthodoxy in line with scripture's canon, and bore witness alongside the body of believers of his time.

Since this is outside the scope of this book, any substantial understanding of these individuals and their work requires your reading and research of the readily available records of history, writings, and commentaries from both religious and secular sources.

Chapter 18

Church Orthodoxy

With this chapter, my initial goal was to identify a point in history that I could reference as an example of unity and modern organization, serving as an anchor of orthodoxy. I aimed to escape history's shabby view of the days of the Apostles and the Martyrs and find evidence of structural development, societal influence, and political standing. For instance, during Constantine's time, councils had a unified voice. In other words, when did the Church establish a globally recognized body as a unified entity? When did we rise to power? And, in a sense, when did we gain pride in this world?

However, I realized that the more we are represented through mere terrestrial values and intellectual frameworks, the further we move away from the organic growth of the Faith and, therefore, from its true representation as it ought to be. What do I mean by "as it ought to be"? Orthodoxy, Ecumenism, and Canon have been at the center of history's debate to prove Catholicity among the churches. Yet, we fail to recognize that we have carried the terminologies with us in carnal values while abandoning the essence of the terms through our divisions.

Orthodoxy is preserved by the Apostolicity of the Church, regardless of the Church's numerical and territorial growth. Its structural model and authoritative guidelines were patterned after Christ and modeled by the Apostles. Scripture was completed and confirmed as penned by them or authorized by them. The Presbyterian system of governing the Church, which was passed on to the Apostolic Fathers, was sanctioned by God, as was Scripture, and modeled within Scripture through the same apostolicity. Neither Papal See nor imperial alliances, orthodoxy claims, renewed that authority for any power of amendment to the Apostolic establishment. Nowhere did Scripture propose apostolic succession as endowed with the authority of Christ beyond the twelve Apostles, including Paul. On the contrary, Scripture specifically points out that such authority is borne witness to by the signs of apostleship.

"The things that mark an apostle, signs, wonders, and miracles, were done among you with great perseverance" (2 Corinthians 12:12).

Ecumenical or Ecumenism, as far as the faith is concerned, represents its global body regardless of the number of its members throughout the inhabited world or their locations. That statehood and membership of the Church represent Christ to the world. However, lack of knowledge and improper teaching are often imbued with certain biases that are ingrained within specific schools of thought. These biases support their branding and schism, rather than being objectively open to the truth and bound by scripture. To avoid those biases and remain within the rules of scripture, we adhere to what is known as the Canon of the Bible, as prescribed and inspired by the Holy Spirit.

Canon

There are numerous studies and works of scholarship regarding the canon of Scripture that are more comprehensive than I can provide. Therefore, it would be unkind of me to compile or format data for you when better and more gifted resources are available for the benefit of the Body. One of those resources, which I believe is second to none, is a teaching series by Michael Kruger, "The New Testament Canon," available at [Ligonier Ministries] (https://www.ligonier.org/learn/series/).

In this series, he raises the question of the Achilles heel of Canon: Why do we believe in these 66 books and no others? He addresses three tributaries to this problem:

Claims of forgeries: Are the authors of the New Testament really who they claim to be?

Discoveries: Books discovered in archaeological excavations, such as the Book of Thomas.

Scholarly influence: Scholars like Walter Bauer argue that early Christianity was widely diverse, with each branch having its own theology, and we merely inherited the theology of the victors.

Mr. Kruger noted that his approach to starting the series with these problems was to allow us to feel the tension surrounding these debates.

The next series focused on Canon's definition, stating that our understanding can influence the date we assign to Canon, regardless of whether we are examining the same historical evidence—it's a definition shaped by one's worldview. He outlined three complementary definitions that, when considered individually, present a distorted view, but together provide a comprehensive understanding:

1. The exclusive definition: A fixed, final, and closed list, dating the Canon to the fourth century. This gives the impression that the Church remained in the dark for four centuries and only established a canon because of some action taken.
2. The functional definition: Books are being used authoritatively as scriptures. Therefore, we can date the Canon to the 2nd century.
3. The ontological definition: The books that God gave His Church. By this definition, we can date the Canon to its conclusion, which was when the last book was written, around 98 AD, when John wrote Revelation.

He explained how the first and second definitions are problematic:

They depend on the Church to begin using them authoritatively or to formulate them. The third definition asserts that the books had authority, regardless of what the Church did or knew, because they were given by God. With these definitions, although it took time to solidify the Canon, there was a canon from the moment those books were written.

Mr. Kruger argued that the reason for the Canon was innate to the early Christian faith, rather than a development imposed on the Church. He based his conclusion on three doctrinal beliefs:

1. Fulfillment of the Old Testament: The story of the Old Testament was completed in the life and teaching of Jesus of Nazareth. The Jews of the first century continually looked forward to the promises made in the Old Testament.
2. New Covenant: Jesus fulfilled the promises of the Old Testament and established a New Covenant. Jewish Christians from a covenant background expected a written document to accompany the New Covenant; thus, the Canon is a natural outcome.
3. Apostolic Authority: The teachings of the Apostles were regarded with the same authority as those of Christ.

In this series, Mr. Kruger delves into the validity of these claims from both historical and scriptural perspectives, continuing with lectures on

"The Date of the Canon," "The Authors of the Canon," and "The Attributes of the Canon."

In Mr. Kruger's sentiments, the Apostles were very explicit in their admonitions, quotations, and affirmations of their writings as authoritative and scriptural. They were followed by the early Church Fathers, most of whom I discussed in the previous chapters.

- Regarding "The Attributes of the Canon," I would like to express this. A growing frustration as I became a believer was the countless instances of debate over the meaning of scriptures or things clearly stated in scripture that seemed unclear to many. My greater frustration was the conflict among fellow believers over texts and their inability to discern between erroneous and sound doctrine or to recognize the truth. I am not being presumptuous, boastful, or judgmental; I understand that we can all be clouded in our judgment or deceived at times. However, this is why we have the indwelling of the Holy Spirit, enabling us to discern and recognize the truth, if we are His.
  For example, some time ago, I had to rebuke two mature believers who seemed to abandon their resolve regarding the sufficiency and completeness of the Bible's 66 books. They began to entertain speculations from a nonbeliever attempting to persuade us of the validity of the Apocryphal books and conspiracies about the Jews tampering with the translations of the Bible.
  After my conversion, I had a "New Catholic Bible" that included those books: 1st and 2nd Maccabees, Sirach, Wisdom, etc. Initially, Sirach and Wisdom seemed similar to Proverbs, but I began to recognize their differences, although I dismissed my awareness of the consensus in the Canon. As I became more familiar with scripture, it became clear that they were not scripture. Another realization was that the Holy Spirit played a crucial role in helping me make that distinction. I could listen to a preacher and discern the truth or deviations from the truth

without knowing theology. I understood that the Holy Spirit, as the Spirit of Truth, not only recognizes truth but also reveals it with conviction against falsehood.

"It is the Spirit who gives life; the flesh is no help at all. The words that I have spoken to you are spirit and life." John 6:63 (ESV)

Mr. Kruger declared Canon's divine quality based on its excellence and living efficacy. And equally important is the need for the recognizer to be alive, to acknowledge that life. Canon or Scripture is by the Spirit of Life and therefore alive, but one must have the Spirit to recognize life within it. To the question, "Is there a reliable way to recognize scripture in our modern age?"

He said resoundingly, "Yes! By reading it." Its divine qualities of beauty and excellence enable you to see and hear Christ if you are His sheep. Its power and authority will convict, rebuke, encourage, and come alive in you. The unity and harmony of 66 books from 40 different authors, spanning diverse backgrounds and over five thousand years, tell one story of an eternal God and humanity's salvation. It is analogous to distinguishing a poem from a monkey randomly typing keys on a typewriter.

In essence, Canon was never dependent on human counsel or even the Church. It is the Word of God: The Laws and the Prophets, the Old and New Testaments or Covenant decrees, written by the Holy Spirit through the instrument of men, borne witness by the indwelling of the same Spirit in men and women called of God in Christ Jesus.

However, human nature, always prone to error, highlights the need for an ecumenical representation to clarify and distinguish opinions among individuals. As the Church grew, the necessity for a body of standards, established through councils and edicts, emerged. The first council, held in Jerusalem around AD 50, decreed that Gentile Christians were exempt from observing the Mosaic Law. Many more councils followed over the centuries, which I believe remained faithful to orthodoxy until the 6th century, at the Third Council of Constantinople, leading up to the 9th-century split.

As the Apostles left the scene, the body of believers continued to grow across the Greco-Roman world. The need for greater coherence in expressing and defending the faith increased as the contrast between Christian ideals and the demands and conflicts of pagan culture, religious mysticism, and politics heightened. The upheaval of slander and persecution against Christians dominated the first three centuries, while heresies and doctrinal controversies called for great defenders and theologians.

God allowed the floor of these controversies in man's rebellion and tenacity to exhaust all plausible arguments against the truth, so that history may record a body of doctrines affirmatively expressed by canon and apostolic faith.

The focus is on doctrinal history, but we need the context of the political and violent persecutions of that era.

In the summer of 64, Nero rounded up all the Christians he could find in Rome as scapegoats for a fire that burned much of the city, and the citizens subjected them to cruel deaths. Shortly afterward, it officially became a crime to be a Christian. They were gossiped about and slandered, accused of cannibalism, sexual promiscuity, and incest. They were blamed for every misfortune since they rejected the pagan gods, who were believed to bring prosperity and protection. This treatment continued into the 2nd and 3rd centuries under Pliny the Younger, governor of Bithynia, and Emperor Trajan (AD 111); and later, Emperor Decius (AD 249 –251). From 257 to 259, Emperor Valerian attempted to eradicate church leaders, but after being taken prisoner in war, his son Gallienus issued an edict of toleration.

In February 303, co-emperors Diocletian and Galerius initiated significant persecution that lasted until 311, under the sole rule of Galerius. He died shortly after concluding it, afflicted by a painful disease.

In 312, Emperor Constantine claimed to have had a vision of the cross in heaven with the inscription, "In this sign, conquer." After he won, he converted to Christianity. In 313, he and Licinius, as co-emperors, issued the Edict of Milan, which granted Christians full legal rights, among other things. Following this, it became popular and eventually prestigious to be a Christian. Consequently, Christianity also became a tool for political gain and influence. Along with these developments, there was only a requirement for a confessional baptism for any citizen to be a member of the Christian Church, to the extent that it was thought Christianity and Rome were synonymous.

Meanwhile, the successors of the Apostles and early Church fathers continued to uphold the tenets of doctrine and authority by suppressing heresies from within and resisting external opposition.

Councils

Here, I will highlight the first six Ecumenical Councils and examine the historical trajectory to determine how it aligns with or deviates from biblical orthodoxy. This analysis will help clarify the true line of succession of orthodoxy throughout this period of Church history. Then, in the following chapter(s), we will investigate the remaining councils.

1. First Council of Nicaea (AD 325)
Convened by Constantine to address the Arian heresy, which questioned the divinity of Christ, it confirmed that Christ is "begotten, not made, of one substance (homoousios) with the Father."

It also laid the foundation for future Christological debates and the understanding of the Trinity by formulating the Nicene Creed, which affirmed the consubstantiality of the Son with the Father.

Nicene Creed:

- *We believe in one God, the Father Almighty, Maker of all things visible and invisible.*
  And in one Lord Jesus Christ, the Son of God, begotten of the Father, the only begotten; that is, of the essence of the Father, God of God, Light of Light, very God of very God; begotten, not made, being of one substance with the Father; by whom all things were made, both in heaven and on earth;
  who for us men, and for our salvation, came down and was incarnate and was made man; He suffered, and the third day He rose again, ascended into heaven; from thence He shall come to judge the quick and the dead.
  And in the Holy Spirit.

2. First Council of Constantinople (AD 381)

Called by Emperor Theodosius I, this council condemned Arianism, Apollinarianism, and other heresies; affirmed the doctrine of the Trinity (Father, Son, and Holy Spirit); and further unified the Church's theology on Christ's full divinity and humanity.

Key Outcome: Expanded the Nicene Creed to affirm the divinity of the Holy Spirit:

- *We believe in one God, the Father Almighty, Maker of heaven and earth, and of all things visible and invisible.*

  And in one Lord Jesus Christ, the only-begotten Son of God, begotten of the Father before all worlds; Light of Light, very God of very God; begotten, not made, being of one substance with the Father; by whom all things were made.

  Who, for us men and for our salvation, came down from heaven, and was incarnate by the Holy Spirit of the Virgin Mary, and was made man; He was crucified for us under Pontius Pilate, and suffered and was buried; and the third day He rose again, according to the Scriptures; and ascended into heaven, and sits on the right hand of the Father; and He shall come again with glory to judge the quick and the dead; whose kingdom shall have no end.

  And in the Holy Spirit, the Lord and Giver of Life; who proceeds from the Father; who with the Father and the Son together is worshiped and glorified; who spoke by the prophets.

  And in one holy catholic and apostolic Church. We acknowledge one baptism for the remission of sins. We look for the resurrection of the dead, and the life of the world to come. Amen.

3. Council of Ephesus (AD 431)

The council addressed the Nestorian controversy regarding Christ's nature. Nestorius, the Patriarch of Constantinople, taught that Christ's human and divine natures were distinct, opposing the term Theotokos (Greek, "God-bearer" or "Mother of God"). He suggested Christotokos ("Christ-bearer" or "Mother of Christ") instead, claiming it was theologically incorrect to refer to Mary as Theotokos, which implied that she gave birth to the divine nature.

He taught that the divine and human natures were joined yet remained distinct. This view raised questions about whether Christ was one person or two coexisting persons, one human and one divine.

Cyril of Alexandria argued that Christ's human and divine natures were united in one person without division, emphasizing the hypostatic union. He also insisted that Mary bore the entirety of Jesus Christ, fully God and fully man.

The council condemned Nestorius' teachings and issued anathemas against his views, resulting in his exile. Some Eastern churches rejected the council's decrees, leading to a schism and contributing to the formation of the Assyrian Church of the East.

The council affirmed the hypostatic union, which became foundational to Christology. Christ was acknowledged as one person with two natures—divine and human—united without confusion, change, division, or separation.

Proclaiming Mary as the Theotokos (God-bearer) and affirming the unity of Christ's divine and human natures shaped the Church's understanding of Mariology and Christology.

4. Eutyches, an abbot from Constantinople, responded to Nestorius' teachings by overemphasizing the unity of Christ's nature, teaching that Christ's humanity was so united with His divinity that it was essentially "dissolved" or "absorbed." This suggested that Jesus' humanity was altered or diminished, raising the question of whether Christ can fully represent humanity if His humanity is not distinct. This doctrine, known as Monophysitism (from Greek mono, meaning "one," and physis, meaning "nature"), denies Christ's true humanity by claiming that after the Incarnation, Christ had only one nature. In 448, Flavian, the Patriarch of Constantinople, condemned Eutyches' views locally. However, the attention drawn by the debate prompted Emperor Theodosius II to convene the Second Council of Ephesus in 449, which sided with Eutyches and reinstated him. This council, which later became known as the "Rubber Council," was not recognized by most

of the Church and was subsequently repudiated by the Council of Chalcedon, the Fourth Ecumenical Council.

The Council of Chalcedon (AD 451)

After the death of Theodosius II, Emperor Marcian and Pope Leo I convened a new council to address the Eutychian controversy and the nature of Christ. The council condemned Eutychianism and Monophysitism, affirming that Christ's divinity did not absorb his humanity and asserting that Christ's human and divine natures coexisted fully and distinctly. This council formulated the Chalcedonian Definition: "Christ is one person in two natures" (dyophysitism), fully divine and fully human, without confusion, change, division, or separation. Christ's two natures exist in a hypostatic union—that is, they are united in one person while remaining distinct. The Tome of Leo: The letter written by Pope Leo I to Flavian of Constantinople significantly influenced the council's decision. He emphasized that Christ is fully God and Man, with both natures in one person.

5. Many Eastern churches, including the Coptic, Armenian, and Syrian Orthodox Churches, rejected the council's definition. These churches adhered to a Miaphysite Christology, which proposes that Christ's divine and human natures are united in a single nature, but without the extreme absorption concept attributed to Eutyches that led to the Fifth Council.

Second Council of Constantinople (AD 553)

Convened by Emperor Justinian I to address ongoing theological disputes related to Christology, particularly concerning the lingering controversies surrounding the Nestorian and Monophysite positions and the interpretation of the Council of Chalcedon (451), this council condemned the Three Chapters, along with certain writings and teachings considered Nestorian. These include Theodore of Mopsuestia, who held Nestorian ideas that emphasized the distinction between Christ's human and divine natures; Theodoret of Cyrus, who critiqued Cyril of Alexandria and was associated with Nestorianleaning theology; and Ibas of Edessa, whose letter to Maris defended Nestorius while criticizing Cyril. Its reaffirmation of the Chalcedonian Definition clarifies that condemning the Three Chapters was not a condemnation of Chalcedon but a rejection of lingering Nestorian interpretations. The council further elaborates on the hypostatic union, with Justinian playing a significant role in the theological discussions and influencing the emphasis on the unity of Christ's two natures in one person, countering the tendency toward dualism (Nestorianism) or Monophysitism. Additionally, the council issued anathemas against Origen's cosmology, his views on the preexistence of souls, and, ultimately, his teachings on the restoration of all things, including the Devil.

6. Tensions persisted between Chalcedonian Christians, who believed in Christ's two natures, and non-Chalcedonian (Miaphysite) Christians, who argued for a united nature. To reconcile these divisions, Byzantine emperors proposed new formulas to find common ground without compromising Chalcedonian orthodoxy. While affirming Christ's two natures, they suggested that He operated with a single divine will, leading to the emergence of Monothelitism.

Patriarch Sergius I of Constantinople initially promoted Monothelitism – that Christ had "one divine-human will." Pope Honorius I of Rome endorsed Sergius' proposal. Maximus the Confessor argued that denying Christ's human will undermines the fullness of His humanity. He insisted that true salvation required Christ, as fully human, to possess a genuine human will that cooperated with His divine will. He emphasized that while Christ's human and divine wills were distinct, they were perfectly aligned, with the human will submitting to the divine will in voluntary harmony, which led to the Sixth Council.

Third Council of Constantinople (AD 680-681)

Also known as the Sixth Ecumenical Council, this council was convened by Emperor Constantine IV to address Monothelitism definitively. The council condemned Monothelitism as heretical, affirming that Christ possessed two wills (dyothelitism): one divine and one human, consistent with His two natures. It was declared that these two wills were in perfect harmony, with Christ's human will freely submitting to His divine will. The council reinforced the Chalcedonian Definition by emphasizing that Christ's two wills existed in a true hypostatic union without confusion or division. The council also condemned later figures associated with Monothelitism, including Patriarch Sergius and Pope Honorius.

The Deformation of Orthodoxy

Bear in mind that our Lord's patience means salvation, just as our dear brother Paul also wrote you with the wisdom that God gave him. He writes the same way in all his letters, speaking in them of these matters. His letters contain some things that are hard to understand, which ignorant and unstable people distort, as they do the other Scriptures, to their own destruction. — 2 Peter 3:15-16

The Church's struggle to balance spiritual authority with temporal power stems from two enduring issues: heresy and humanity's relentless pursuit of control. Under the guidance of the Apostles, these challenges were managed with spiritual focus and discipline. However, what happens when the Church no longer stands apart but merges with the state, wielding temporal power alongside spiritual authority? Constantine's cessation of Christian persecution marked a pivotal moment in the history of the Church. While his support liberated the Church from external oppression, it simultaneously shifted its focus from a heavenly mission to earthly governance. Church leaders, once shepherds of a persecuted flock, now found themselves navigating the complexities of state-like authority. This newfound prominence diluted the purity of the Church's spiritual mission, as it increasingly mirrored the structures and ambitions of an earthly kingdom. The Church's transcendence—its unique calling as a holy and separate body—became entangled with the world's political systems. Under apostolic foundations, it operated distinctly, guided by the Spirit, and focused on spiritual authority. However, as it ascended to societal prominence, jurisdictional conflicts and doctrinal disputes emerged, particularly between Rome and Constantinople. This shift diluted its distinct witness and laid the groundwork for centuries of tension.

Chapter 19

The Rise of Iconography and the Second Council of Nicaea

Initially, the Church adhered strictly to the Second Commandment's prohibition against graven images, distancing itself from both idolatry and the surrounding pagan culture. Early Christians used simple symbols such as the fish (Ichthys) and the Chi-Rho, not as objects of veneration but as educational tools. These symbols helped sustain Christian identity and faith during persecution without violating Scriptural commands.

By the fourth and fifth centuries, however, icons gained prominence in both Eastern and Western traditions. No longer mere tools for instruction, they evolved into objects of veneration. Proponents of iconography argued that these images facilitated a connection with the divine and provided a means of grace. Figures like John of Damascus and Theodore the Studite defended icons by invoking the doctrine of the Incarnation: since Christ made the invisible God visible, it was deemed acceptable to depict Him visually.

This growing practice sparked significant controversy during the eighth century's Iconoclastic Controversy. Iconoclasts, or "image breakers," condemned icons as idolatrous, urging a return to the purity of worship commanded in Scripture. In contrast, Iconodules (supporters of icons) argued that these images were valuable aids for devotion and teaching. The debate escalated under Emperor Leo III, who ordered the removal of icons, citing idolatry and interpreting military defeats as evidence of divine displeasure.

The controversy culminated in the **Second Council of Nicaea** in 787. Here, the Church formally endorsed the veneration of icons, distinguishing between latria (worship due to God alone) and dulia (veneration offered to saints and angels). Proponents argued that icons served as visual aids for devotion, not objects of worship. However, this distinction introduced a theological complexity that was absent from Scripture, which unequivocally reserves worship for God alone:

"You shall not make for yourself a carved image... You shall not bow down to them or serve them" (Exodus 20:4-5).

While defenders of icon veneration sought to avoid idolatry, their practices blurred the line between reverence and worship. The council's decisions marked a shift in orthodoxy, replacing the simplicity of Scriptural commands with complex theological distinctions. This response to cultural pressures redefined worship, moving it away from biblical truth.

The Fourth Council of Constantinople and Ecclesiastical Authority

The Fourth Council of Constantinople (869-870) sought to reconcile divisions between the Eastern and Western Churches. It deposed Photius, a prominent Eastern bishop, and reinstated Ignatius as Patriarch of Constantinople. However, the council's underlying tensions revealed a deeper power struggle between Rome and Constantinople. The issues debated—ranging from icon veneration to papal primacy—illustrated the growing divergence between the two traditions.

Also, this council's hierarchical approach differed from the servant-leadership model exemplified by Christ. Jesus explicitly taught against adopting worldly power structures:

"The rulers of the Gentiles lord it over them... Not so with you. Instead, whoever wants to become great among you must be your servant" (Matthew 20:25-26).

By embracing centralized authority and endorsing the veneration of icons, the Church moved further away from the humble, Spirit-led governance of the apostolic era. This trend deepened divisions that culminated in the Great Schism of 1054, fracturing the unity for which Christ prayed in John 17:

"That they may all be one, just as you, Father, are in me, and I in you, that they also may be in us, so that the world may believe that you have sent me" (John 17:21).

Marian Veneration and Theological Expansion

The Council of Ephesus (431) proclaimed Mary as Theotokos ("God-bearer"), affirming Christ's dual nature as fully human and fully divine. While this doctrine upheld Christological orthodoxy, it inadvertently elevated Mary's status. Over time, practices such as hyperdulia—a unique form of veneration reserved for Mary—developed, surpassing the biblical honor due to her as the mother of Jesus (Luke 1:42-48).

Scripture emphasizes worship centered on Christ, cautioning against the elevation of created beings, including saints, angels, or Mary:

"Worship God!" (Revelation 22:9).

The distinctions between latria (worship), dulia (veneration), and hyperdulia (unique honor for Mary) reflect human attempts to reconcile tradition with Scripture. However, these practices risk leading believers into idolatry, replacing the simplicity of faith with man-made constructs.

Division and Disunity: A Fragmented Body

The East-West Schism revealed the tragic consequences of the Church's entanglement with worldly power and authority. The Roman Catholic Church's emphasis on papal primacy and the Eastern Orthodox Church's conciliar model exemplified their divergence. Both traditions claimed orthodoxy, yet both deviated from the unity that Christ desired for His Body.

Paul's exhortation to avoid divisions (1 Corinthians 1:10) and Jesus' prayer for unity (John 17:21) underscore the Church's calling to remain one, distinct from the world. However, divisions often reveal areas of disobedience and immaturity within the Body, prompting believers to seek repentance and reconciliation.

The deformation of orthodoxy is a historical phenomenon and an ongoing challenge. When human tradition replaces Scriptural truth, the Church loses its distinct witness. Only by returning to the simplicity and purity of the Gospel can the Body of Christ fulfill its calling as a holy, united people.

Chapter 20

Forged in Conflict

"Keep watch over yourselves and all the flock of which the Holy Spirit has made you overseers. Be shepherds of the church of God, which he bought with his own blood. I know that after I leave, savage wolves will come in among you and will not spare the flock. Even from your own number men will arise and distort the truth in order to draw away disciples after them." - Acts 20:28- 30

As stated earlier, when Christianity rapidly expanded across the Greco-Roman world after the passing of the Apostles, the Church faced increasing challenges from pagan culture, religious mysticism, and political pressures. The first three centuries were marked by persecution, slander, and doctrinal controversies, necessitating strong theological defenses. God permitted these conflicts to arise, resulting in a definitive body of doctrine grounded in apostolic faith and Scripture.

Persecution intensified under emperors such as Nero (AD 64), Trajan (AD 111), Decius (AD 249–251), and Diocletian (AD 303–311), as Christians faced accusations of crimes and were targeted for their refusal to worship pagan gods. Temporary reprieves, like Gallienus' Edict of Toleration, offered some relief, but severe oppression continued until Emperor Constantine's conversion in 312 AD. The Edict of Milan (313 AD) granted Christians legal rights, rendering Christianity both socially advantageous and susceptible to political exploitation.

Amid these trials, early Church Fathers and apostolic successors worked to preserve doctrinal integrity, combat heresies, and defend the faith, ensuring the Church's theological and structural foundation remained strong.

Distinctions of the Body and Authority

"Without pre-fixing consulate, month, and day, they wrote concerning Easter, 'It seemed good as follows,' for it did then seem good that there should be a general compliance; but about the faith, they wrote not, 'It seemed good,' but, 'Thus believes the Catholic Church;' and thereupon they confessed how they believed, in order to show that their own sentiments were not novel, but Apostolical."
— **Athanasius, *De Synodis***

In the early Church, there were no distinctions within the Body; it was inherently separate from the world. The Apostles referred to the Church as a singular, universal entity: "...to the saints which are at Ephesus," emphasizing its unity across all nations in the name of the Father, Son, and Holy Spirit. When Paul addressed divisions within the Body, he acknowledged their necessity: "So that those who are approved may be recognized among you" (1 Corinthians 11:19). Here, heresies (Greek: hairesis) and divisions (schisma) indicated disunity or sectarianism, highlighting the Church's struggle to maintain doctrinal unity. The line of division often manifests in two ways: Speculative Thinking—conjectures based on human reasoning that attempt to fit God into finite frameworks, revealing an unregenerated heart; and Religious Convictions—rooted in transcendent faith, demonstrated in Christ through divine revelation and the Spirit's influence. The most significant historical controversies often centered on the authority and nature of the Godhead, culminating in debates about Christ's divinity. However, God used these conflicts to accomplish His purposes. Throughout history, whether confronting heresies like Gnosticism,

Montanism, or Arianism, or facing external persecution, the Church has been refined by God's providential hand.

The First Divide

The first major schism in Church history culminated in the East-West division, formally marked by the Great Schism of 1054. This division arose from centuries of theological, cultural, and political tensions. The Roman Catholic Church became increasingly centralized under papal authority, forming close ties with Western European powers. It was characterized by doctrinal changes, such as the inclusion of the Filioque clause, and distinctive liturgical practices. The Eastern Orthodox Church, rooted in a conciliar governance model, upheld its traditions, including the original Nicene Creed and Byzantine liturgical practices. Earlier controversies, such as the Iconoclast Controversy, had already underscored the growing divide. The Fourth Council of Constantinople (869 AD) aimed to heal these divisions. However, it could not resolve the ongoing power struggles between East and West, which were fueled by doctrinal disagreements and political ambitions.

Chapter 21

The Springboard of Power and the Medieval Era

With the legalization of Christianity, there was an influx of converts motivated by social and political prestige. The church's worldly influence and human leadership increased, but this was accompanied by a troubling moral decline and some of the most heinous atrocities committed in the name of Christianity. This shift in the Church, from being persecuted to waging holy wars, prompts deep questions. Did the Church of Jesus Christ, against which He declared, "the gates of hell shall not prevail," fall into corruption and follow the rules of hell? Or did the adversary, disguised as an angel of light, build global institutions falsely claiming to be the Universal Church?

And what I am doing, I will continue to do, in order to undermine the claim of those who would like to assert that in their boasted mission, they operate on the same terms as we do. For such men are false apostles of Christ. And no wonder, for even Satan disguises himself as an angel of light. (2 Corinthians 11:12-14)

Is it just a coincidence that the sins of unbelief, idolatry, and rebellion, which led Israel to judgment and exile, mirror the actions of the Second Council of Nicaea? Has the faithful Israel of God once again wandered into a spiritual wilderness due to rebellion?

But even if we or an angel from heaven should preach to you a gospel that is contrary to the one we preached to you, let him be accursed. - Galatians 1:8

The widespread story that the Pope's inherited apostolic authority is based on a misinterpretation of scripture and the baseless claim that the Church of Rome is the true Church of Jesus Christ. For such a claim to be valid, it must align with biblical precedent and demonstrate the results of the Gospel. This misuse of scripture weakens the true teachings of Christ.

The Roman Catholic Church continues—not as the triumphant body of Christ but as a symbol of the broad road, the spiritual Ismael born of rebellion. Its existence acts as a test, revealing heresies so that "they which are approved may be made manifest among you."

As the medieval Church expanded, it diverged from the Orthodox Church due to cultural and political influences, adopting a centralized, hierarchical structure that deviated from the New Testament model of church leadership. This divergence raises concerns and warrants a critical examination of the Church's development.

In the days of the Apostles and the early Church Fathers, the Episcopal model was dominant: local bishops (episkopoi) served as overseers alongside presbyters (elders) and deacons (Acts 14:23; 1 Timothy 3:1-13; Titus 1:5-9). Authority was shared among bishops, who had local autonomy and a group of elders (1 Peter 5:1-3; Acts 20:17-28). Leadership is based on Christ's humility and service, with Him as the ultimate head (Ephesians 5:23).

The Roman persecution strengthened unity among Christians, with the church in Rome assuming a coordinating role due to its prominence. By AD 96, Clement's letter to the Corinthians showed Rome's influence, even though it didn't have universal authority.

The Edict of Milan (AD 313) legalized Christianity, boosting Rome's importance alongside Alexandria, Antioch, Jerusalem, and later Constantinople. Later councils reaffirmed a hierarchy, giving special recognition to Rome.

Doctrinal Controversies and Papal Influence

The Council of Chalcedon marked a turning point, with Pope Leo I's Tome defining Christ's dual natures. Soon after, Rome reinforced its claim to Peter's primacy through Matthew 16:18-19. This council was an important event in the history of the Christian Church, as it clarified the nature of Christ and His relationship with God the Father. Rome's bishops asserted their succession from Peter, which sparked opposition from the East.

After the fall of the Western Roman Empire in AD 476, the Bishop of Rome became a stabilizing figure. Pope Gregory I (6th–7th centuries) strengthened papal authority, protected Rome, and increased missionary efforts. His title, "servant of the servants of God" (servus servorum Dei), hid the consolidation of power.

The fall of the Western Roman Empire did not mark its end; instead, it turned into the Papal States.

Rome's association with Peter and Paul grew into a claim of supremacy. However, this connection, based on political influence, lacks biblical and historical proof. The roots of the Papacy reflect totalitarianism politically and heresy theologically.

The Papacy's authority stemmed from Rome's political power rather than its church legitimacy. The idea that Peter and Paul's martyrdom established Rome's dominance has no scriptural evidence. Christ, crucified in Jerusalem, is the true foundation of the Church, implying that Jerusalem, not Rome, should have primacy.

The Foundations of the Papacy: Power, Lies, and Alliances

The development of the Papacy rests on three main pillars: political power, forged documents and false claims, and alliances with worldly kingdoms. These elements combined to form an institution that shaped medieval Christendom and continues to impact global history and modern geopolitics. This exploration traces the rise of the Papacy through key historical milestones and documents, critically examining its foundations.

Political Power

The transformation of the Church into a political entity began with a key moment in history: Constantine's conversion and his alliance with the Church. Following the Edict of Milan in 313 AD, which legalized Christianity, the Church gained significant political influence. As the imperial capital, Rome naturally became the center of church authority. The Council of Nicaea (325 AD) accorded the bishop of Rome special respect, laying the groundwork for the development of papal supremacy. By the fifth century, the bishop of Rome had become a major voice in doctrinal debates. The impact of Pope Leo I's Tome of Leo was crucial in shaping Christological doctrine at the Council of Chalcedon (451 AD). The fall of the Western Roman Empire in 476 AD further enhanced the Pope's status, as the Bishop of Rome assumed both spiritual and political leadership to fill the power vacuum. The 7th century saw the rise of papal influence through figures like Pope Gregory I (also known as Gregory the Great), who reformed church administration and sent missionaries, such as Augustine of Canterbury, to spread Christianity among the Anglo-Saxons. Gregory's efforts laid the groundwork for the medieval Papal States. A major milestone in the rise of papal power occurred in 751 AD when Pope Stephen II allied with Pepin the Short. Pepin's anointment as King of the Franks reinforced the idea that kingship needed papal approval. This relationship reached its peak with the Donation of Pepin, which granted the Pope control over central Italy. Charlemagne's coronation as Holy Roman Emperor on Christmas Day in 800 by Pope Leo III further strengthened the political role of the papacy. This alliance revived the Western Roman Empire and emphasized the Pope's authority to crown and depose emperors, a power later confirmed by Pope Gregory VII's "Dictatus Papae" in 1075.

The Donation of Constantine: Forgery

One of the most infamous forgeries supporting claims of papal temporal power was the Donation of Constantine. This eighth-century document claimed that Emperor Constantine transferred authority over the Western Roman Empire to Pope Sylvester I as a gesture of gratitude for the latter's healing of the former from leprosy. Although Lorenzo Valla exposed it as a forgery in the 15th century, the Donation of Constantine had long been used to justify papal territorial ambitions.

The Dictatus Papae, issued by Pope Gregory VII, further reinforced these claims by asserting the Pope's authority over secular rulers and the infallibility of the Roman Church. Some of its main declarations included:

"That the pope alone can with right be called universal."

"That he alone can depose or reinstate bishops."

"That he has the power to depose emperors."

"That the Roman Church has never erred; nor will it err to all eternity."

These claims positioned the Pope as the supreme authority, capable of absolving subjects from their loyalty vows to kings deemed unworthy. Such declarations laid the groundwork for conflicts, such as the Investiture Controversy, during which Pope Gregory VII excommunicated Emperor Henry IV, forcing him to seek absolution at Canossa in 1077.

Lay Investiture and the Investiture Controversy

Lay investiture, the practice where secular rulers appointed bishops and abbots, blurred the lines between church and state authority. The Papacy's condemnation of this practice reached its peak during the Investiture Controversy, which concluded with the Concordat of Worms in 1122. This agreement created a compromise in which the Church kept the right to appoint bishops with spiritual authority, while the emperor could grant them temporary authority.

Crusades and Justifications of Violence

The Papacy's call for the Crusades further showed its involvement in politics. In 1095, Pope Urban II convened the Council of Clermont, urging Western Christians to reclaim the Holy Land. He promised indulgences and the forgiveness of sins to those who took up the cross. The First Crusade (1096-1099) successfully took Jerusalem; however, later Crusades led to atrocities, including the sacking of Constantinople during the Fourth Crusade (1204), which deepened the split between Eastern and Western Christianity. The Papacy's support for violent campaigns included the Albigensian Crusade (1209-1229), which targeted the Cathars of southern France. This campaign's infamous order, "Kill them all; God will know his own," showed the brutality approved by the Papacy.

Inquisitions and the Suppression of Heresy

The Inquisition institutionalized the persecution of heretics, Jews, and Muslims. Pope Gregory IX's establishment of the Papal Inquisition in 1231 marked the beginning of systematic trials and executions. The Spanish Inquisition, under Ferdinand and Isabella, targeted conversos (Jewish and Muslim converts suspected of relapsing), while the Roman Inquisition aimed to suppress Protestant reformers.

Notable cases include the execution of Giordano Bruno in 1600 and the trial of Galileo Galilei in 1633, highlighting the Church's resistance to scientific progress.

Modern Papacy: Alliances with Political Powers

The Papacy's involvement with political powers persisted into the modern era. Similar to the Lateran Pact of 1929, established between Mussolini and the Holy See, which designated Vatican City as an independent state, thereby ensuring papal neutrality during global conflicts. Pope John Paul II's collaboration with U.S. President Ronald Reagan contributed to the collapse of communism in Eastern Europe, particularly in his native Poland.

The history of the Papacy reveals an institution founded on both political ambition and the manipulation of spiritual authority. While the Roman Church undoubtedly helped preserve knowledge and promote cultural development, the methods it used to gain power often starkly contrasted with Christ's teachings—The Church's true mission, as demonstrated by the martyrs and apologists of the early centuries, calls for humility, service, and unwavering dedication to the Gospel—a clear contrast to the coercive and deceptive tactics that have, at times, characterized the Papacy.

Chapter 22

Reformation

Reform: to improve or eliminate faults. Merriam-Webster defines "reform" as "to put or change into an improved form or condition" or "to amend or improve by changing the form or removing faults or abuses." The Protestant Reformation should be distinguished from earlier efforts at reform, which mainly aimed to refine or restore practices within the established institutions of the Western (Roman Catholic) Church and, to some extent, the Eastern Orthodox Church. These earlier reforms often reinforced institutional authority even while addressing deviations from Scripture. In contrast, the Protestant Reformation marked a break from these institutions, driven by a return to Scripture as the only authority. Those who challenged the institutional norms were called heretics and often faced persecution, exile, or death. A lack of meaningful dialogue through councils or debates further solidified the institution, blocking reform efforts by using political and military power.

The Protestant Reformation was not a split of Christianity into different denominations. Instead, it was a renewal—a return to the biblical roots of the faith and a rejection of institutional traditions and abuses that had clouded the Gospel. Faith is determined not by human institutions or councils, but by the Spirit of God, who provided the Scriptures and illuminated their truths. This divine influence was vital in the Reformation, guiding it back to the authority of Scripture and correcting errors that had crept into Church doctrine and practice.

The term "Reformation" often evokes images of Martin Luther nailing his Ninety-Five Theses to the church door in Wittenberg. However, the Reformation was not merely a historical event—it was a profound theological and institutional upheaval that brought about changes to restore Christianity. Essentially, the Reformation sought to reaffirm the authority of Scripture and rectify the errors that had crept into Church doctrine and practice.

Divine Sovereignty and Institutional Rebellion

Throughout history, despite humanity's tendency to rebel, God has carried out His will through individuals. He created mankind through Adam, established Israel through Abraham, and delivered His people through Moses, only to face rebellion at every turn. Even the Church, founded by Christ through the Apostles by the power of the Spirit, has not escaped this pattern. Disunity within the Body of Christ directly reflects the deceitfulness of the human heart and humanity's inability to please God without the Spirit's guidance. Institutions formed through human effort often foster division instead of unity. Naturally, people come together in groups or institutions to pursue common goals, but this unity stems from the human heart. This dynamic leads to phenomena like crowd psychology and mob mentality. While one might think this should promote unity, it often produces the opposite within the Body.

First, "The heart is deceitful above all things, and desperately sick" (Jeremiah 17:9). Second, "Those who are in the flesh cannot please God" (Romans 8:8). These truths show why human efforts, even within religious institutions, often create divisions instead of unity. True unity in the Body of Christ comes only through the Spirit of God, not through councils, traditions, or institutions. History supports this: from the days of Noah, Pharaoh, and Israel in the wilderness to the heretics and

Judaizers of the Apostolic era, and from Israel's idolatry to the rise of the papacy and its subsequent deviations. Humanity—both individuals and institutions—tends to rebel, reject correction, and face judgment. However, God consistently works through those who are willing to lay down their lives for the truth, guided by the Spirit of Truth.

Throughout history, humanity has consistently tried to redefine faith on its terms. The pattern of rebellion against divine authority is evident from Israel's demand for a king (1 Samuel 8) to the corruption of the medieval Church. The Protestant Reformation was partly a response to these distortions—an attempt to realign with God's sovereign will, as revealed in Scripture, rather than through institutional tradition.

The Intellectual Revolution and Its Consequences
The 12th and 13th centuries marked an intellectual revolution within the Church. The traditional monastic model of theological education, centered on the Church Fathers and Scripture, shifted toward a more scholarly approach. Scholars like Thomas Aquinas sought to integrate Aristotelian philosophy with Christian doctrine, thereby advancing theological discussions, albeit often at the expense of a pastoral and biblical focus. Theology became more abstract, moving away from the simplicity and reverence of popular piety, which was expressed through actions rooted in love and respect. The tension between divine authority and human institutions had been growing for a long time. Wielding great power, the medieval Church often blurred the lines between spiritual leadership and secular authority. This resulted in doctrines and practices that prioritized the ecclesiastical hierarchy over biblical truth, calling for reform. Efforts to address this included the rise of the Mendicant orders, such as the Franciscans and Dominicans. The Franciscans embraced poverty and directly served the poor, following the example of Francis of Assisi. Meanwhile, the Dominicans combined intellectual rigor with a missionary spirit. While these reforms emphasized personal devotion, practical piety, and accessibility for laypeople—mirroring early Church practices—they ultimately remained loyal to the Church institution.

The Renaissance and the invention of the printing press played crucial roles in spreading biblical literacy. The ability to print and distribute Bibles in the vernacular allowed more people to read Scripture in its original languages, revealing discrepancies between Church teachings and the Bible's clear messages. This intellectual awakening, fueled by the spread of knowledge, was both a blessing and a challenge—it empowered reformers but also created divisions as different interpretations emerged. As theological inquiry flourished, so did the risk of division. The rise of humanism, which emphasized individual reasoning and sometimes led to prioritizing personal interpretation over collective orthodoxy, was a major factor in the Reformation. Therefore, the Reformation was both a fight against corruption and a test of unity within biblical truth.

Corruption and Reform Movements

The 14th and 15th centuries presented major challenges to the Church and the papacy. The crises of the Avignon Papacy, which moved the papacy from Rome to Avignon, the subsequent Western Schism that created multiple claimants to the papacy, and the devastating Black Death led many to question traditional religious explanations and authorities. These crises sparked reform movements within the Church and more radical challenges to its authority. Figures like John Wycliffe in England and Jan Hus in Bohemia emphasized the authority of Scripture, criticized the Church's wealth and power, and pushed for vernacular translations of Scripture to make God's Word accessible to everyone.

After the early Church gained social prominence, the institutional Church became more involved in political, financial, and military matters. Corruption, greed, and deception have troubled the Church since at least the eighth century. Examples include the papal claim of infallibility, the building of the Vatican, the Crusades, and the Inquisitions—all actions that starkly contrast with the faith's teachings. While hypocrisy is a common human flaw, the "staggering hypocrisy" of these institutions often revealed that many men involved were likely not true Christians. As Scripture says, "By their fruits, you will know them" (Matthew 7:16).

The problem persists because institutions like the Roman Catholic Church have established themselves as global political and economic powers. By creating their own traditions, often conflicting with Scripture, and forming alliances with governments, they have protected themselves from accountability. Though their abuses may seem unchecked in this world, the consequences reach far beyond what is visible.

Despite corruption within institutions, God has consistently raised up individuals to stand for the truth. Figures like John Wycliffe and Jan Hus in the 14th and 15th centuries challenged widespread corruption and paid a heavy price for their convictions. Their bravery, however, inspired greater resistance to the spiritual tyranny of their time. By the 16th century, Martin Luther's bold stand against unbiblical practices sparked the Protestant Reformation, transforming Europe's religious landscape.

John Wycliffe, an English theologian, was among the first to challenge the wealth and power of the clergy. He advocated translating the Bible into common languages, making it accessible for ordinary people. His teachings inspired the Lollards, a reform movement that continued despite opposition. Building on Wycliffe's influence, Jan Hus, a Czech preacher, openly condemned church corruption and the moral failings of the clergy. For his defiance, Hus was excommunicated and ultimately burned at the stake. His martyrdom sparked the Hussite Wars, marking a significant milestone in the growing resistance to church oppression.

In 1517, Martin Luther took a critical step in this movement when he nailed his Ninety-Five Theses to the door of Wittenberg Church. His defiance sparked the Reformation in Germany, challenging the sale of indulgences and other corrupt practices. By 1520, Pope Leo X excommunicated Luther, and in 1521, he was declared an outlaw at the Diet of Worms. During this turbulent time, Luther translated the New

Testament into German, making Scripture accessible to ordinary people.

Before Luther, figures like John Wycliffe and Jan Hus called for reform, challenging the Church's reliance on extrabiblical traditions and papal authority. Their efforts faced strong opposition, but they laid the groundwork for reformation. Luther's message resonated with audiences in a Europe weary of clerical abuses and indulgences when he appeared.

Luther's focus on Sola Scriptura (Scripture alone) and Sola Fide (faith alone) challenged the Church's authority at its core. His ideas, disseminated widely by the printing press, quickly reached others and inspired reformers such as John Calvin, Ulrich Zwingli, and John Knox. Each sought to restore biblical truth in their own way, though their interpretations sometimes led to doctrinal disagreements.

The Reformation expanded beyond Germany. In Geneva, John Calvin emphasized the doctrine of predestination and God's sovereignty. His major work, 'Institutes of the Christian Religion,' became a cornerstone of Reformed theology. Calvin also established a theocratic government in Geneva, turning the city into a center for reform.

Meanwhile, in Switzerland, Huldrych Zwingli led the Reformation in Zurich. He supported the authority of Scripture and opposed Catholic practices such as venerating saints and using images in worship. In Scotland, John Knox established Presbyterianism, which was strongly influenced by Calvinist principles. Throughout Northern Europe, the movement developed in different ways, with Lutheranism becoming the primary form in Denmark, Norway, and Sweden.

The core of the Reformation was not to create new denominations but to restore faith by bringing God's Word back to the people. For centuries, the institutional church had kept the masses in lies and silence. Reformers like Wycliffe and Luther faced harsh persecution because they aimed to make the Scriptures accessible. The Roman Church enforced its traditions and wielded its power to maintain control, insisting on its authority over the interpretation of God's Word.

The history of the Church consistently shows this struggle. As Jesus promised, the gates of hell would not overcome His Church (Matthew 16:18). Still, the Church's victories are not measured by earthly successes but by the blood of martyrs. From the early Church to the Reformation, believers have continued to testify to Christ's victory over death, hell, and the grave through their faithful endurance.

In France, the Reformation gained traction among the Huguenots, who faced harsh persecution, most famously during the St. Bartholomew's Day Massacre of 1572. Similarly, in England, Mary I tried to restore Catholicism through brutal persecution, earning her the nickname "Bloody Mary." In response to the Reformation, the Catholic Church launched the Counter-Reformation. Although it aimed to address internal corruption, the Council of Trent (1545–1563) ultimately reaffirmed Catholic doctrines, deepening existing divisions.

The Reformation also caused major conflicts. In Germany, the Peasants' War (1524–1525) highlighted the social and political implications of the religious reform movement. The Thirty Years' War (1618–1648), one of the deadliest conflicts in European history, ended with the Peace of Westphalia. This treaty ended the war and established the principle of cuius regio, eius religio ("whose realm, his religion"), which allowed rulers to choose their state's religion. It also marked the decline of the Holy Roman Empire's dominance.

Since the Reformation, many nations and denominations have adapted their faith in response to the beliefs of their leaders. Unfortunately, some have continued to manipulate Scripture to serve their own purposes. For example, the Charismatic Prosperity Gospel distorts the biblical message by emphasizing materialism. Likewise, the Episcopal Church, despite its Anglican roots, has retained many structural and doctrinal elements of the Roman Church. These deviations remind us that efforts to suppress the truth through tradition and religious oppression did not end with the Reformation but persist even today.

These ongoing assaults on the truth are part of the spiritual war described in Scripture. As Paul writes:

"For we do not wrestle against flesh and blood, but against the rulers, against the authorities, against the cosmic powers over this present darkness, against the spiritual forces of evil in the heavenly places" (Ephesians 6:12).

The fight for truth, carried on by Wycliffe, Hus, Luther, and many others, is not just a historical battle — it continues to unfold today. Still, the Word of God stays strong, and the victory belongs to Christ alone.

The Theological Core of the Reformation

The Reformers rallied around five key doctrines known as the Five **Solas**: Sola Scriptura, Sola Fide, Sola Gratia, Solus Christus, Soli Deo Gloria.

These principles were more than just academic distinctions; they marked a return to the biblical foundation of faith. They directly challenged a system that centered on human mediation, tradition, and merit in salvation—fundamentals that are the roots of Protestantism.

The term "Protestant" comes from the "Protestation" at the Diet of Speyer in 1529, when several German princes and cities opposed an imperial decree aimed at suppressing the reforms started by Martin Luther and his followers.

Key Characteristics of The Reformation and Protestantism

- **Sola Scriptura (Scripture Alone):** Scripture alone is the highest authority. Protestants hold that the Bible is the only authoritative source for Christian faith and practice. This principle dismisses the authority of church traditions that contradict or supplement Scripture's teachings.
- **Sola Fide (Faith Alone):** Justification, or being made right with God, is by faith alone, not by works. This principle emphasizes that salvation is a gift from God received through faith in Jesus Christ rather than earned through human efforts.
- **Sola Gratia (Grace Alone):** Salvation is solely by God's grace, not earned through human actions. God's grace is the unmerited favor that brings salvation to the sinner.

- **Solus Christus (Christ Alone):** Jesus Christ serves as the sole mediator between God and humanity. Salvation is achieved through Christ's sacrificial death and resurrection, thereby negating the need for other mediators, such as saints or priests.
- **Soli Deo Gloria (Glory to God Alone):** Every part of life and faith should be lived exclusively to honor God. This principle rejects any form of human boasting or self-glorification in matters of religion, as well as glory attributed to saints, Mary, or angels.

The debate among unbelievers about whether the Bible is the Word of God is never-ending. However, this matter is settled for believers: The Spirit who dwells within bears witness to His Word, as He moved chosen men to write it. Still, we often forget that other men are also influenced in this cosmic war, albeit by the spiritual forces of evil in the heavenly places. If, as 1 Corinthians 12 tells us, we were easily led by dumb idols when we were pagans, how much more can wicked men be compelled to write the doctrines of demons? This explains texts like The Book of Mormon by Joseph Smith or more insidious distortions, such as The New World Translation by Jehovah's Witnesses, which falsely claim to "correct" Scripture—an outright blasphemy! Likewise, the Catholic Church elevates its traditions and doctrines to the level of Scripture, while others manipulate Scripture to support their ideologies under the guise of "interpretation."

The hallmark of true reformation is a return to the unilateral authority of the Bible, which is self-sufficient, self-interpreting, and authenticated by the Holy Spirit.

Personal Reflection and the Ongoing Call to Reformation

The Reformation was not just a historical event but an ongoing challenge to align our faith with God's truth. Each generation faces the temptation to compromise, to replace divine authority with human traditions, and to accept a faith shaped more by culture than by Scripture.

True reformation begins not only with theological debates but also in the hearts of believers who seek God's will above all else. Just as the Reformers stood firm against corruption and false teaching, we too must hold fast to the Word of God in our time.

History shows us that revival happens whenever God's people return to His Word. The Reformation was one such revival, and the need for reformation remains today.

After my regeneration, I spent many years among Pentecostal circles and non-denominational charismatics, as these movements dominate my cultural and environmental context. From the beginning, however, my deep hunger for truth drove me to study the Bible and seek understanding wherever I could find it. I encountered John Calvin's Institutes of the Christian Religion early in my search. I remember thinking, "This isn't Calvinism; this is simply what the Bible says." Yet, over the years, I have not recognized when or how I became part of the broader Christian and Evangelical world that instinctively disdains Calvinism. For most, this disdain is not a deliberate choice, but an environmental predisposition—a cultural stigma attached to the doctrine.

What we often refer to as Calvinism is also widely known as Reformed or biblical theology. However, it took me a considerable amount of time to understand this. The point is that environment and culture can act as powerful and persuasive blinders. For a believer, the Bible is not just an intellectual puzzle to be analyzed by scholars. It is accessible to even the most ordinary person, while offering a depth that even the most insightful scholar can explore. It is neither allegorical nor subjective, and it does not depend on human mediation. It is not subject to personal interpretation but calls for obedience. Will you understand everything immediately? No, but that is why God provides sanctification.

I didn't figure all of this out on my own; much of it came from painful and unnecessary experiences. However, as I grow older, the truth becomes more attractive and compelling. The irony of spiritual growth is that just when you think you are starting to understand, you realize how much you still do not know. Over the years, I encountered programs like Renewing Your Mind with Dr. R.C. Sproul. Although the Christian television networks of that time, such as TBN, often promoted questionable doctrine, Sproul's teaching motivated me to conduct a doctrinal checkup. With the rise of the internet and social media, resources have become more accessible. I found like-minded truth in Ligonier Ministries and its affiliates. For me, Dr. Sproul became a filter for reliable biblical teaching.

This leads me to an important point: reformation is not about aligning with a particular branch or school of thought. It is about returning to the truth and removing distractions and veils. Paul's warning in Galatians is clear: "If anyone—even an angel—preaches a different gospel, let him be cursed." Today, the Church is troubled by forms of Christianity motivated by greed and pride. However, culture remains one of the most significant obstacles for those genuinely seeking the truth. Often, the obstacle isn't outright bias, but rather perceptions formed by cultural and religious conditioning.

Consider, for example, when I discovered John MacArthur. At first, I disliked listening to him. Finishing his message went against my preferences. However, now I listen to him second only to Dr. Sproul. This change taught me an invaluable lesson: the Spirit of God is not limited by culture or religious background. He cares only about the truth in Christ, which is clear and absolute in the text of Scripture.

Some may argue that we are living in a more dangerous era than the medieval period. While we no longer face the suppression of the Holy Roman Empire, we contend with a proliferation of institutions under the guise of reform, many of which have strayed far from the principles of the Reformation. From the world's perspective, this confusion might seem justified. They cannot truly know God. Those who do acknowledge His existence often settle for religious platitudes, whether they identify as Christian or not. Some, using basic logic, admit that only one sovereign and universal God can exist. However, even this acknowledgment often leads to a false prejudice, as they claim their god is the true one.

What is truly astonishing is what we see within mainstream Christianity today. Many claim to follow the same scripture, yet they are divided into irreconcilable factions. These divisions are not just due to disagreements over difficult passages or theological nuances; they stem from established practices and customs that conflict with one another. How can there be multiple conflicting interpretations of the same text? The Bible is clear, from Genesis to Revelation, that there is one God, one hope, one faith, and one salvation. Therefore, only one interpretation can be correct. This is not a matter of love or tolerance, but rather a matter of logic.

The Reformation and Protestant movement aimed to return to the Bible. It started with the effort to make the Word accessible. The Logos—reason and logic—refers to those who interpret the Word literally. This does not mean we can perfectly obey every part of Scripture all at once. Growth, whether intellectual or spiritual, takes time. However, as we grow, this should lead to greater unity within the Body of Christ. Divisions caused by customs or ideologies that deviate from the plain text of Scripture are not signs of growth or calling; they are products of human doctrines.

Chapter 23

The Problem of Little Faith

As discussed in Section 1, the search for the Will of God is often driven by anxiety, pride, a longing for special knowledge, the pursuit of signs and wonders, or even unbelief. Ironically, the fall of Mankind started with the temptation to be like God: "For God knows that when you eat from it, your eyes will be open, and you will be like God, knowing good and evil," said Satan.

In Matthew 16:1, when *"the Pharisees and Sadducees came, and to test Jesus, they asked him to show them a sign from heaven,"* but he said to them, *"... An evil and adulterous generation seeks for a sign, but no sign will be given to it except the sign of Jonah."*

In Christ's sentiments, the only sign pointing to the will of God that we should look to or be concerned with is the sign of Jonah. Or as termed in our religious identity, the sign of the cross: Christ crucified, and on the third day, he rose from the dead. He said it like this, *"For this is the will of my Father, that everyone who looks on the Son and believes in him should have eternal life, and I will raise him up on the last day."*

I believe the main problem or reason for our ongoing effort to uncover some hidden mystery beyond the simple gospel and scriptures lies in our teaching and doctrines. Which, in turn, impacts our understanding of the faith and, consequently, its nature.

Matthew chapters 16 and 17 can shed some light on this. After the Pharisees and Sadducees tried testing Jesus in chapter 16. *"When the disciples reached the other side, they had forgotten to bring bread. And Jesus said to them, '**Watch and beware of the leaven of the Pharisees and Sadducees**,' and they began to discuss among themselves, saying, 'We brought no bread.' But Jesus, aware of this, said, '**O you of little faith**, why are you discussing among yourselves the fact that you have no bread?'"* Matthew16:5-8.

Two charges encapsulated Jesus' tutorship of his disciples: it is the charge of having "little faith," in Matthew 16:8 and 17:20. However, they are not the same.

In Matthew 16:5-8, he addressed their need to perceive and understand the truth correctly by warning them against the incorrect teaching of the Pharisees and Sadducees. Ironically, in that very lesson, their response displayed the need to correct the measure of their faith. Instead of trusting God and grasping what is important, they are still anxious about bread, despite previous proof of His provision.

The Greek, oligopistoi – from oligos (small, little, few), and pistis (faith): "little-faith ones" or "those of insufficient faith." Conveys not a weakness in power, meaning a small quantity of faith that is powerful, but rather a lack of trust - a failure to trust in what God has said and already proven, or to forget what you have seen of God and cannot draw the proper conclusion. This is similar to what is addressed in the earlier chapters, by the renewing of the mind, as commanded in Romans 12:1-3, and growing through the "till" process to draw proper conclusions for obedience of faith.

In Matthew 17:20, the context is entirely different. After attempting and failing to cast out a demon, Jesus rebuked the demon, healing the boy instantly. Afterwards, they asked him, *"'Why could we not cast it out?' He said to them, 'Because of your little faith.'"* In this case, Jesus acknowledged their faith; likewise, they also expected to cast out the demon. So they asked, "Why couldn't we?" Their problem was not a lack of conviction or anxiety about the wrong things, but the nature of their faith.

The Greek, oligopistia, literally means "littleness of faith" or "smallness of faith." The nuance here is that the faith was ineffective, but Jesus qualifies it by saying, even *"if you have faith like a grain of mustard seed, ... nothing will be impossible."* It was ineffective because it lacked the reality of genuine trust to act in God's power.

In Mark, the same account was given from a different narrative. In this case, the boy's father's faith comes into question. *"Jesus said to him, 'If you can'! All things are possible for one who believes."* (ESV). The father also had little faith, though slightly different, resting on Jesus' word. "All things are possible for one who believes." Though his faith was weak, he confessed, "I believe," and acknowledged his weakness in dependence, "help my unbelief!" That trust and humility, in reliance on Jesus' ability to help his unbelief, is the mustard seed.

As a believer, I eventually stopped worrying about what I would eat, wear, or where I would live. In my station in life, as with most people, if I do not trust God daily, my life becomes a mountain of anxiety, as do unbelievers. However, with my regeneration, along with those initial experiences of God's provision beyond what I could hope for in my natural circumstances, it grew from a tiny seed. If our call had ended with regeneration, I could have slept peacefully, waiting to go on to glory.

Nevertheless, we are called as ambassadors of Christ and given gifts for the benefit of the whole Body. This is where the mustard seed faith comes into play, especially regarding the gifts of the Holy Spirit. These gifts are not the same as receiving a gift in the natural world. Naturally, after receiving a gift, it is up to us to decide how to use it. It now belongs to me and is left to my discretion for my purposes. However, as believers, the gift remains the Holy Spirit's and is still subject to His plans and purposes.

What does that have to do with mustard seed faith? Everything. The little faith in Matthew 17:20 reflects a failure to trust and rely on God. I have a gift, and for years, I have analyzed and evaluated it to figure out how to use and apply it. I am just now realizing that the gift is not mine to assess and apply; God sovereignly uses His gift, showing proof of its benefit through that realization. Our responsibility is to trust in His power, which can only start as a mustard seed.

Now, let us look at the middle ground. Between the anxiety despite God's provision in Chapter 16, verse 8, and trusting in His power to act through faith, there is the development of faith over time, including its content and nature. In Chapter 15, we discussed Peter's confession, which is the foundation of the church, coming immediately after Jesus warned about the teachings of the Pharisees and Sadducees. However, regarding Peter's confession, Jesus told his disciples not to tell anyone that he was the Christ. I believe that, as His chosen, this faith was intrinsic to their apostleship, but for the rest of us, who come to faith through their testimony, it was destined for the gospel after the resurrection. Immediately afterward, in verse 21, Jesus predicts His death and resurrection.

"From that time Jesus began to show his disciples that he must go to Jerusalem and suffer many things from the elders and chief priests and scribes, and be killed, and on the third day be raised. And, Peter took him aside and began to rebuke him, saying, 'Far be it from you, Lord! This shall never happen to you." (Matthew 16:21,22 ESV)

Leaven of Pride and Elitism

The story of the disciples in Matthew 16 and 17 reflects our struggles with faith, pride, and humility. Essentially, this passage warns us that illumination, even when given by God, is never the fullness of truth. Our understanding of revelation must always be approached with humility, or else we become the source of distortion within the Body of Christ.

When Jesus warned His disciples, "Beware of the leaven of the Pharisees and Sadducees" (Matthew 16:6), He was warning about a danger that still exists in the Church today. The Pharisees valued their traditions highly, and the Sadducees relied on worldly reasoning. Both distorted God's Word, binding people to elitist systems that replaced God's voice with their own.

So it has been for generations. Some become proud and build on the initial revelation of the Holy Spirit. Enamored by the gift and its wonder, they are overtaken by pride. They never pause to consider that, no matter how great God's deposit in their lives, it is still only a glimpse of the eternal. He has not entrusted the complete revelation to any one individual but to the entire Body. To insist otherwise only leads to division rather than truth. This elitism grows more common when doctrine is influenced by culture and philosophy instead of the eternal Word of God. We see the same problem in our churches when leaders claim illumination comes only through them, depriving the Body of edification. Jesus called such distortion "leaven," because like yeast, it silently works through the whole, producing corruption.

Nevertheless, in the same chapter, Peter stands as proof that God reveals truth directly to His people. When he confessed, *"You are the Christ, the Son of the living God"* (Matthew 16:16), Jesus declared, *"Flesh and blood has not revealed this to you, but My Father who is in heaven."*

This reminds us that Christ Himself is the source of faith, and the Spirit who testifies to the truth is the seal of faith. Faith is based on divine revelation, not human intellect, cultural persuasion, or clever frameworks. However, Peter's confession was not the complete truth; it was only a glimpse. Our danger is to cling to a partial revelation as if it were full. Like Peter, many receive genuine insight but stumble when they think their part is the whole. Immediately after his great confession, Peter rebukes Jesus for predicting His death (Matthew 16:22). In pride, he mistakes a glimpse of glory for the complete plan of God. Jesus' sharp rebuke— "Get behind me, Satan"—shows the danger of becoming messengers of Satan when we try to build on revelation without humility.

Similarly, in the Church, leaders can elevate themselves by sharing fragments of truth, using their position as a shield against correction. Revelation without humility turns into presumption, and presumption can cause division.

The Call to Deny Self

Jesus followed this rebuke with the timeless call: "If anyone desires to come after Me, let him deny himself, and take up his cross, and follow Me" (Matthew 16:24). Here lies the remedy for our pride and division: self-denial.

Our divisions are rarely disputes of faith, but of doctrines of leaven and therefore little faith. Ministers who should foster unity have instead built elitist systems that elevate themselves above the Body. Their philosophy claims illumination comes only through them, but Christ says discipleship begins with death to self. The wisdom of men exalts intellect, charisma, or tradition; the wisdom of God demands humility, love, and sacrifice.

The Glimpse of Glory

The Transfiguration in Matthew 17 demonstrates the same lesson. On the mountain, Peter, James, and John saw Christ in brilliant glory, with Moses and Elijah by His side. Overwhelmed by the vision, Peter suggested building tabernacles, as if the experience itself were the main purpose.

However, the Father interrupted: "This is My beloved Son... listen to Him" (Matt. 17:5). The glory was not meant for display but to strengthen their faith for the suffering ahead.

Our encounters with God, no matter how wondrous, are only glimpses. They point us back to Christ, not to our pride. When we hold onto the gift instead of the Giver, we risk freezing faith in one moment and missing God's bigger work.

The Problem of Little Faith

Coming down the mountain, the disciples failed to heal a boy tormented by a demon. Jesus explained, *"Because of your little faith"* (Matt. 17:20). Their failure was not from lack of effort, but from lack of prayerful dependence on God.

This scene speaks to our condition as well. Some, though true in the faith and even established in ministry, remain stuck in ignorance and pride. They may build platforms and amass resources, but in the infancy of faith, they are humbled before all. God exposes their immaturity, sometimes even allowing others to call them frauds. In a sense, it is true—not that their faith is false, but that their knowledge and sanctification are still in infancy.

Faith must never rest in human frameworks or worldly wisdom. It abides only in dependence on the Spirit, for He alone convinces, testifies, and brings God's Word to life.

The Humility of Christ

The chapter closes with a striking picture of humility. Though the Son of God was free from obligation, Jesus paid the temple tax "lest we cause them to stumble" (Matthew 17:27).

This act demonstrates the very principle missing in much of our leadership today: humility for the sake of love. Christ chose submission rather than asserting His right, setting the pattern for His disciples to follow.

So too must the Church. Structures, doctrines, and offices have their place, but they must never overshadow love or replace the liberty of the Spirit. True unity comes not from asserting superiority, but from humbling ourselves and seeking love above all.

Revelation without humility leads to pride, or as Paul says, knowledge puffs up. Pride leads to division, and division deprives the Body of edification. The antidote is continual repentance, a faith rooted not in intellect or culture but in dependence on the Spirit, and a love that supersedes position or doctrine.

The faith that abides will determine the hope that shines. The hope that shines will manifest in the unity and holiness of God's people, and the love that endures will preserve the Body until the fullness of Christ is revealed.

Illumination

God illuminates great men and communicates certain truths of His Word, and they use this illumination to bring truth and religion into coherent doctrines for contemporary living. This work of theology has often served as a gift to the Church, for it provides order, language, and structure to faith that might otherwise remain unarticulated. However, illumination does not equate to infallibility. The truths they gather and systematize must always remain subject to the higher authority of the Word itself.

Paul reminds us, "we prophesy in part, and we know in part" (1 Cor. 13:9). Doctrines, no matter how noble, share in that partiality. They are not eternal in themselves, but temporary scaffolding meant to aid the believer's understanding of the eternal Word.

The problem arises when those doctrines are treated as a priori truths or become points of contention when they do not cover every practical particularity. What was meant to be a servant of faith often becomes its master, and doctrines harden into boundaries of exclusion, drawing lines between brethren where Christ has not drawn them.

This was not unlike the error of the Pharisees, who exalted traditions and interpretations to the level of divine command (Mark 7:8–9). Instead of guiding people toward God, their system became a stumbling block. Likewise, when doctrinal formulations are absolutized, they no longer serve to lead believers into maturity but rather divide them.

It is understood that every Word is given with a measure of faith, and doctrine or contemporary teaching cannot add to the Word but only serve as our harness to understanding it. Faith responds directly to the Word of God, not to the formulations of man. As Paul says, "faith comes by hearing, and hearing by the word of Christ" (Rom. 10:17).

Doctrine, at best, is a lens. It may focus the eye of faith upon the truth, but it is never itself the source of sight. When treated rightly, doctrine provides a framework for discipline and order, but when treated wrongly, it becomes a substitute for living faith.

Doctrines, then, function as our harness to Scripture—necessary at times, but never sufficient. A harness restrains and guides, but it cannot give life. The Spirit gives life, and the Word breathes faith into the heart.

This distinction is seen in Christ's rebuke to the Sadducees: "You are mistaken, not knowing the Scriptures nor the power of God" (Matthew 22:29). They had their interpretations and doctrinal positions, yet because they missed the life of the Word, they missed the power behind it. In like manner, doctrines must always be tested against the living witness of Scripture and the Spirit, lest they become dead forms.

Doctrines are necessary, but they are not ultimate. When they remain subject to the Word, they edify and unify. When they are exalted beyond scripture, they fracture and mislead. Thus, the call is clear: let us hold to the Scriptures as the fountain of faith and let doctrines serve only as tools to guide us in obedience to the will of God.

In the final essence, the will of God is not the pursuit of our task to complete, but the resolve of the entire body, a final resolve that binds our conscience together. God becomes the first, the only, and the final source, where it is not just about your calling or obedience, but your dependence on Christ, and all these things will be added, "that God may be all in all." (1 Cor. 15:28.)

www.ingramcontent.com/pod-product-compliance
Lightning Source LLC
Chambersburg PA
CBHW070816120626
46556CB00002B/527